# Going Deeper

A devotional for couples wanting to go deeper with God and each other

Liz Gregg and Darrell Cocup

First published 2021.

Scripture quotations marked [NIV] are taken from the Holy Bible, New International Version®, Copyright ©1973, 1978, 1984, 2011 by Biblica, Inc.® Used by permission. All rights reserved worldwide.

Scripture quotations marked [PT] are taken from The Passion Translation®. Copyright ©2017, 2018 by Passion & Fire Ministries, Inc. Used by permission. All rights reserved. www.thepassiontranslation.com.

Scripture quotations marked [NLT] are taken from the Holy Bible: New Living Translation. 2015. Carol Stream, IL: Tyndale House Publishers. Used by permission. All rights reserved.

Scripture quotations marked [NASB] are taken from the Holy Bible: New American Standard Bible. Copyright ©1995. LaHabra, CA: The Lockman Foundation. Used by permission. All rights reserved.

Scripture quotations marked [ESV] are taken from The ESV® Bible (The Holy Bible, English Standard Version®), Copyright ©2001 by Crossway, a publishing ministry of Good News Publishers. Used by permission. All rights reserved.

Scripture quotations marked [NKJV] are taken from the New King James Version®. Copyright ©1982 by Thomas Nelson. Used by permission. All rights reserved.

Other Sozo for Couples resources include:
The Sozo for Couples manual
Starting Out, Marriage Preparation for Couples
Sozo for Couples Foundations eCourse

For details of these and other Sozo for Couples resources visit
www.sozoforcouples.org

Typesetting by Wizard Communication

## Thanks

We are always overwhelmed by the trust that couples put in us when they come for ministry. They really do put their lives in our hands. This book is for them, and for every couple who recognise that "Going Deeper" is what God wants for us.

Liz would also like to thank Jonathan Garside for his helpful comments and encouragement.

## Dedication

Liz writes: To my wonderful husband, Stuart, without whom this journey of marriage wouldn't have been so much fun!

Darrell writes: To Anthea and Oli, for not allowing me to grow old.

# Contents

Prologue ....................................................................................7
Day 1    So What is a Biblical Marriage 1...................................9
Day 2    So What is a Biblical Marriage 2.................................13
Day 3    Two into One ............................................................15
Day 4    Communication: Inspirational ....................................17
Day 5    Communication: Intermediate ...................................21
Day 6    Non-verbal Communication.......................................23
Day 7    Building Values..........................................................27
Day 8    Time .........................................................................31
Day 9    Arguing Well..............................................................35
Day 10   Resolving Issues........................................................39
Day 11   Understanding Repair Attempts ..................................41
Day 12   The Enemy Within-Confrontation and Conflict..........47
Day 13   Love Languages.........................................................51
Day 14   Friendship .................................................................55
Day 15   Boundaries 1..............................................................59
Day 16   Boundaries 2..............................................................63
Day 17   Expectations ..............................................................65
Day 18   Sex Life .....................................................................67
Day 19   Soul Ties....................................................................71
Day 20   Dealing with Parents and In-laws ...............................75
Day 21   The Child Effect........................................................79
Day 22   Worship.....................................................................83
Day 23   Spiritual Life – A Three Stranded Cord ......................87
Day 24   Dealing with Differences............................................91
Day 25   Learning to Laugh .....................................................97
Day 26   Juggling Roles .........................................................101
Day 27   Understanding Your Past ...........................................103
Day 28   Getting Rid of the Victim, Abuser, Hero Cycle............107
Day 29   Dealing with Seasons in Life .....................................111
Day 30   Empathy, Sympathy and Compassion...........................115

| | | |
|---|---|---|
| Day 31 | In Sickness and Health | 119 |
| Day 32 | Love | 123 |
| Day 33 | Understanding Masculinity / Femininity | 127 |
| Day 34 | Understanding Roles | 131 |
| Day 35 | Respect and Honour | 135 |
| Day 36 | Vision and Purpose | 139 |
| Day 37 | Dreaming Together | 143 |
| Day 38 | Choosing the "Us" and Still Being "You" | 145 |
| Day 39 | 'Til Death Do Us Part | 149 |
| Day 40 | What's Next? | 151 |
| Appendix I | | 153 |
| Appendix II | | 155 |
| Resources | | 157 |

# Prologue

*Look at you, my dearest darling,*
*you are so lovely!*
*You are beauty itself to me.*
*Your passionate eyes are like gentle doves*

SONG OF SONGS 1 v 15 [TPT]

Marriage is one of the biggest adventures and challenges that we will enjoy, or endure, in our lives. When we look at passages like those in Song of Songs we realise that this coming together of a man and women is meant to be full of anticipation, joy, expectation, delight and fulfilment. However, the reality can be that marriage is mundane, stable, every-day and doesn't live up to the dream of the day we walked down the aisle in a white dress or smart suit.

Some of you reading this devotional will have had a Sozo for Couples session and will have dealt with the issues that have stopped you from enjoying your marriage. The question now is, how do you continue the journey so that what can be mundane turns into an adventure where both of you feel connected to each other and to God? This book is designed to help answer those questions. Each day as you read, pray, make declarations and discuss together we'll be unpacking different aspects of marriage to help you discover deeper truths about each other, your marriage and your relationship with God. Some of these will develop what was brought up in your Sozo for Couples session, if you've had one, others will be new to you. With each we encourage you to take the time to study and discuss the scripture, pray together and ask (and answer!) the questions.

For others who haven't yet had a Sozo for Couples session, that's absolutely fine! You will still enjoy using this devotional to help you

GOING DEEPER

grow in your marriage. You may find that as you look deeper into some of the topics we cover that agreeing and finding resolution together is difficult. If this happens it might be that it's worth you having a Sozo for Couples session to work through these issues.

However you come to be reading this, if you are married and want to grow in your marriage then this is the book for you! It's written with years of marriage experience, pastoral insight and "Sozo for Couples" wisdom on each page. Our heart in writing this is that each day as you read together, pray and discuss you will grow in love, maturity, and be increasingly able to enjoy your own love story.

## DAY 1

# So what is Biblical Marriage? 1

Most of us want to have a Biblical marriage, or we hope that we already have. What do we mean by this? The Bible is full of people who are married – are we meant to copy them as role models? For example Solomon had 700 wives, is that the pattern we are meant to follow? We hope you know the answer to that is "No".

Thankfully, in Ephesians 5, Paul outlines for us what a Biblical marriage is about. If we read this passage, beginning at Verse 21, we see that we are meant to begin all our relationships out of submission to Jesus, then to each other. It's as we submit to Jesus that we find that we are able to submit to others. This is not subservience but a choice to mutually submit to each other. To not put our own needs and desires first but to willingly choose the other person above ourselves. If both a husband and wife do this then everyone's needs will get met. Make no mistake, the Greek is clear that we should submit to Christ, in fact the only active verb in the sentence is 'submit' to Christ. Our relationships should follow on from that initial, all encompassing, submission.

How do we do that in reality? It means that we choose to value and listen to the other person in the way we communicate, make choices, resolve conflict and choose the purpose of our marriage – in other words it affects everything.

Spend a moment to think about the way you value and listen to your spouse. Can you think of some situations where you have (or maybe haven't) done this recently? Is there anything you're aware of that you need to ask your spouse to forgive you for?

If we continue reading that passage in Ephesians we see some other key elements that form part of a Biblical marriage. We see that the relationship between husband and wife mirrors the one between the Church and Jesus. Jesus is the head, but what kind of head is He? Does Jesus dominate and control? No, He lays down his life for us and He serves us. He loves us, He gives us freedom and brings the best out of us. The husband being the head is therefore about being the one who creates a culture where everyone is able to grow, he serves the family for all to succeed. It's not a role of power and dominance but of love, sacrifice and empowerment.

> *"No woman wants to be in submission to a man who isn't in submission to God!"*
> *T D Jakes*

Don't worry, husbands! You will find fulfilment in this too, because as you lay down your life you will find a wife who can fully submit to you, who will serve alongside you and be truly the partner that God made her to be.

Sound too good to be true? Maybe, but it's completely possible, but only as we come together and submit to God's way and not our way! It might seem counterintuitive in a world that tells us we have to make others meet our needs but in the upside-down Kingdom our needs are met as we all submit to Jesus and through Him to each other.

## Read:

[21] *Submit to one another out of reverence for Christ.*

[22] *Wives, submit yourselves to your own husbands as you do to the Lord. [23] For the husband is the head of the wife as Christ is the head of the church, his body, of which he is the Saviour. [24] Now as the church submits to Christ, so also wives should submit to their husbands in everything.*

[25] *Husbands, love your wives, just as Christ loved the church and gave himself up for her [26] to make her holy, cleansing*

*her by the washing with water through the word, [27] and to present her to himself as a radiant church, without stain or wrinkle or any other blemish, but holy and blameless. [28] In this same way, husbands ought to love their wives as their own bodies. He who loves his wife loves himself. [29] After all, no one ever hated their own body, but they feed and care for their body, just as Christ does the church — [30] for we are members of his body."*

EPHESIANS 5 V 21-29 [NLT]

## Pray:

Ask Father God what stops you fully submitting to your spouse. Spend some time processing these things with Him.

## Discuss:

Have the two of you ever felt in submission to each other? How would this change things in your marriage? How would you both feel about that?

## Declare:

Today I willingly submit to You, Lord God.

GOING DEEPER

GOING DEEPER

DAY 2

# So what is Biblical Marriage? 2

Yesterday we read Ephesians 5 starting at verse 21, which is the part that speaks about marriage. However, in the original Greek, the chapter divisions or headers that most of our Bibles have simply weren't there. In the Greek we really need to start further back at the bit about being filled with the Spirit;

> *"Instead, be filled with the Holy Spirit, singing psalms and hymns and Spiritual songs among yourselves, and making music to the Lord in your hearts. And give thanks for everything to God the Father in the name of our Lord Jesus Christ."*
> EPHESIANS 5 18B-21, NLT

This is the instruction Paul gives us as our approach to all the relationships we are to have. It is the big, scene setting, verb that all the other, smaller, verbs fit into. In other words, our marriage relationship should be filled with the Spirit. The Greek is stronger still, requiring us to keep on being filled, on an ongoing basis, not as a one off event, by His Holy Spirit.

The reality is that to make our relationships work we need to be filled with the Spirit. We need the Holy Spirit within us to be able to have a marriage where we don't play power games but learn to submit. We need the Holy Spirit to help us make this new unit together. We need the Holy Spirt so our relationships are full of the fruits the Spirit gives us. Let's remind ourselves about them - love, joy, peace, patience, goodness, faithfulness, gentleness, kindness, self-control — we want to have fruity joy filled marriages!

The impact of this fruit in our marriage should be far reaching, but one of the immediate out-workings should be that we don't compete with each other, vying for the upper-hand. We've probably all witnessed

13

those couples who do this in front of everyone. It's not pleasant to watch, but the truth is that for some of us it wouldn't take too much for us to be the same. Think about those times when you disagree, does it feel more important to win the argument or hear your spouse and understand them? If it feels more important to win then it's time to get full of the Holy Spirit and get more fruity, as there is no room for the upper-hand in a fruity Biblical, Spirit filled marriage!

## Read:

> [21] *But the fruit of the Spirit is love, joy, peace, forbearance, kindness, goodness, faithfulness,* [23] *gentleness and self-control. Against such things there is no law.* [24] *Those who belong to Christ Jesus have crucified the flesh with its passions and desires.* [25] *Since we live by the Spirit, let us keep in step with the Spirit.* [26] *Let us not become conceited, provoking, and envying each other."*
>
> GALATIANS 5 V 22- 25 [NIV]

## Pray:

That you will have more fruit of the Spirit in your marriage. Pray to be filled up daily with the Holy Spirit.

## Discuss:

How does reading today's message make you feel? Would either of you like a better relationship with Holy Spirit? What difference do you feel it would make?

## Declare:

You delight to encounter me. Your eye is on me and you are waiting to pour in Your presence and power.

## DAY 3:

# Two into One

*For this reason a man will leave his father and mother and be united to his wife, and the two will become one flesh.*

GENESIS 2 V 24 NASB

This is the mystery of marriage, that what was two separate people now become one flesh. This isn't just about the physical reality of what happens during sex but is a Spiritual reality about how we are now seen by God.

The plan for a Biblical marriage is that we become one unit, separate from both of the families that we have come from, able to make our own choices together. It might seem simple but in reality many newlyweds find this really difficult. Perhaps, in your own marriage one of you is still very connected to a parent and discusses things with them rather than each other. It's just a thought!

The Biblical model is that we should choose to communicate with our partner first, talking things through with them and, together, deciding the way forward. This may lead to us jointly recognising that one of our parents has the expertise, knowledge or wisdom that we need, and we can then jointly approach our parents as being that wise resource. That's a very different approach to putting a parent's opinion above our spouse's.

## Read:

> [31] For this reason a man will leave his father and mother and be united to his wife, and the two will become one flesh. This is a profound mystery – but I am talking about Christ and the church. [33] However, each one of you also must love his wife as he loves himself, and the wife must respect her husband."

EPHESIANS 5 V 31-33 [NIV]

## Pray:

Spend some time praying for a new understanding of what being one flesh really means. Ask God to show you any ties you may have that get in the way of this in your marriage.

## Discuss:

How do you feel about the relationship your spouse has with her/his parents? Do you now or have you ever felt threatened by this? Or annoyed? Is there anything either of you need to change?

## Declare:

I am one, with my partner, before You. We will live and make choices as one unit.

DAY 4

# Communication: Inspirational

Danny Silk says, "In a respectful relationship, each person understands, 'I am responsible to know what is going on inside me and communicate it to you. I do not expect you to know it, nor will I allow you to assume that you know it. And I will not make assumptions about what is going on inside you'"[1]

We have identified three basic levels of communication in any couple's relationship. It is important in every relationship that each of these levels is present to make it fulfilling and to enable us to feel connected with each other.

These are:

**Informational** – This is the kind of communication most of us do on a daily basis. We tell our partner when we are going to work, chat about who needs to pick up the kids or put out the bins. It's the day-in and day-out conversation that makes up a lot of what we say. It is important for the communication and exchange of information but doesn't do much to connect us on a deeper level.

**Intermediate** – This is more about what we might be thinking or planning in the next six months or year. For example, what holidays we are going to take, plans we may have for work or how to manage our money.

**Inspirational** – This communication meets our deeper need to be heard and understood. In Inspirational communication, we speak about our hopes and dreams and our deep thoughts about feelings and issues. We listen to our partner and reflect on their thoughts. Understanding our partner at this deeper level will affect the choices we make at the

[1] Danny Silk *Keep your Love on* Red Arrow Media P100

intermediate and informational levels of communication. This is where we are vulnerable and open. Asking questions such as, "Where would you like to be in five years?" or "What would you do with a £/$1m?" can help this communication.

Now reflect on your relationship. Do you make time for each of these types of communication? It's often easy when we first get to know someone to communicate at an inspirational level. Then, as time passes, we can think, "This is less important now, we know all we need to know". That's not true! To feel deeply connected with someone we need to keep sharing our heart and thoughts. We do this by really opening up and making time for each of these different levels of communication. Inspirational communications can help us do that. The truth is that each of us is constantly changing. The person we met, however long ago, isn't the person you are married to now. What they dreamed and thought about then has changed. Think about yourself – the dreams you had at 20 years' old are not the same as you will have at 50 or 70! As life changes us, some of those dreams will be fulfilled and others won't, but you will have new experiences that will change what you think and feel.

It's good to reflect on how to have this deep communication and to plan to include it in your life together. It's lovely if it happens spontaneously but for most of us life is busy and unless we plan it just won't happen.

## Read:

10  *Now I know that I am filled with my beloved*
    *and all his desires are fulfilled in me.*
11  *Come away, my lover.*
    *Come with me to the faraway fields.*
    *We will run away together to the forgotten places*
    *and show them redeeming love.*
12  *Let us arise and run to the vineyards of your people*
    *and see if the budding vines of love are now in full bloom.*
    *We will discover if their passion is awakened.*
    *There I will display my love for you.*
13  *The love apples are in bloom,*
    *sending forth their fragrance of spring.*
    *The rarest of fruits are found at our doors—*
    *the new as well as the old.*
    *I have stored them for you, my lover-friend!*

SONGS OF SONGS 7 V 10-12 TPT

## Pray:

Either thank God for your deep connection with each other, or ask Him how He wants to help you connect in new and deeper ways with your spouse.

## Discuss:

How do you both feel, reading this? Does "inspirational" communication come naturally to you both? What do you want to do about it?

## Declare:

I am excited that I keep growing and changing and commit to sharing my dreams and visions with my partner. I will avidly listen to their hopes and dreams.

GOING DEEPER

GOING DEEPER

DAY 5

# Communication: Intermediate

Yesterday we looked at the three 'I's of communication and focused on the Inspirational. Most couples, unless communication has completely broken down, include some informational communication in their relationship. Why do some of us find it difficult to do the intermediate? Surely such short term planning should be easy?

The reason it isn't is that topics such as holidays, money and how we spend our time often bring up underlying issues of mismatched values in us. One of us may think that spending money on extravagant holidays is a must, whilst for the other saving for a rainy day is more important. It's not that either of these things is wrong but they do show the mismatched values that we can have.

How do we get over this? Being honest in our communication can be a good start. Instead of reacting to a suggestion that makes no sense to you, stop and ask your partner; "Why do you think that's a good idea?" or "What brings you to make that choice?"

Understanding your own or your partner's values can make it easier to get to the place where you can find a way to create a new, joint, value system for your marriage or for your partner to come aboard with your value.

The next time you're going to talk about money, time or holidays instead of rushing to the details of the planning why not ask each other, "What made you suggest that?" or "What would it mean to you if we did that?" or "What childhood dream or unmet need is it fulfilling?"

## Read:

*"When hope's dream seems to drag on and on,*
*the delay can be depressing.*
*But when at last your dream comes true,*
*life's sweetness will satisfy your soul."*

PROVERBS 13 V 12 <sup>TPT</sup>

## Pray:

About the areas of communication where you feel you haven't heard each other and ask God to show you the mismatched values you have had. For example,

Father God what areas of communication have I not heard my partner well in? Father God can you show me the value behind each of our points of view?

## Dicuss:

How does reading today's message make you both feel? Is there something that now would be a good time to talk to each other about?

Why not have a look at the questions on the Communications Tool Sheet taken from the Sozo for Couple manual? You find these in the Appendix I on Page 95.

## Declare:

I plan well for the medium term by communicating clearly my intentions and values.

## DAY 6

# Non-verbal Communication

Here's a question. When you think about communication, what's the first thing that pops into your head? Is it conversation and speech, or is it, maybe, writing and newspapers? Communication is all about conveying a message isn't it, but it doesn't have to be done in words. Did you know that if you're sitting in a room with a group of people most of what they communicate to you will not be in words? As humans we give out, we transmit messages all the time, and we're programmed to receive messages all the time too, and the point is we hardly know we're doing it. Non-verbal communication then, what isn't said, is every bit as important as what is. In fact between a husband and wife it can be even more so because whilst what is spoken can only really mean the words said, non-verbal communication can carry many meanings. A look or a shrug can mean many things, and of course it's down to the receiver of that look or shrug to translate the meaning, and the likelihood is that they'll do this based on their perception of the state of the relationship at that moment and how they're feeling generally.

Why are we highlighting this? It's because non-verbal communication is very powerful. Between a couple in love, highly tuned into each other's body language and thinking, the slightest movement or look can convey intense meaning, with each of these tiny events somehow deepening the relationship as two hearts beat as one.

Now let me reiterate what you've just read slightly differently. A couple who have been together for a long time become highly tuned to each other's body language and thinking so that even the slightest movement or look can seem to convey intense meaning, with each of these deepening the distance between them as two hearts that once beat as one increasingly dig a chasm between them.

Don't let it happen! Don't use non-verbal communication to be cruel or to punish each other; the sideways glance, the look away, ignoring the offered hand, the passive withdrawal of those secret love-communications you share. There's a hiddenness in non-verbal communication that is beautiful when done in love but hateful and un-Godly when not. We wouldn't suggest you do this in public, but if you feel there's something wrong then at the first private opportunity find out from your partner what's going on and talk it through.

## Read:

> *A worthless person, a wicked man, goes about with crooked speech, winks with his eyes, signals with his feet, points with his finger, with perverted heart devises evil, continually sowing discord;*

> PROVERBS 6 12-14 ESV

> 1   *A gentle answer deflects anger,*
> *but harsh words make tempers flare.*
> 2   *The tongue of the wise makes knowledge appealing,*
> *but the mouth of a fool belches out foolishness.*
> 3   *The Lord is watching everywhere,*
> *keeping his eye on both the evil and the good.*
> 4   *Gentle words are a tree of life;*
> *a deceitful tongue crushes the spirit*

> PROVERBS 14 V 1-4 NLT

## Pray:

Ask Father God to show you times that you have used non-verbal communication in a negative way with your partner. Repent of these times and ask God to show you new ways of brave communication.

## Discuss:

How has it made you feel when your partner has used non-verbal communication in a negative way? Talk about how you can communicate clearly with each other in a private setting.

## Declaration:

I choose to honour my partner in all the ways I communicate and to show love in the way I act, maintaining connection even when it is difficult.

GOING DEEPER

DAY 7

# Building Values

If you got someone else to describe you as a couple, what would they say? Would they say "fun" or "hospitable" or "caring", "hard-working" or "conscientious"?

What would you like them to say? Our values, what we stand for, should underpin and determine what kind of marriage we have. As a couple it's important to build values that you share and live from. Understanding what values are important to you should affect your choices and reduce conflict. For example, if you have decided that you value hospitality and that you will fulfil this by inviting people to your home for Sunday lunch, you shouldn't then be upset when people are in your home!

It's helpful to think about the values that were instilled in us as we grew up. Was your home hospitable or private, was it experiences or possessions that were important? Are those values the ones you want to live up to in your own marriage? What other kind of values do you want to have around your home and family (if you have children). What should your values and priorities be when it comes to work, leisure, finance, church, your relationship together and separately with God?

If you have never done it then it can be helpful to sit down and think through each of these areas and talk about what is important to you both. This will help you discover what your true values are. Once we understand our values, and why we have them, we can then decide if we want to keep them.

Let us explain, you may have been brought up in a home that was always hospitable, with lots of visitors. While this seemed fun to others, this open house policy may have made you feel overlooked and ignored. As a result, you may have always wanted a home that was a place of retreat, of your own, where you are valued and have a voice. Your partner may have also come from a hospitable home but one where he/she was included in conversation, activities with visitors and where their needs were recognised and considered important. He/she may not feel the same need for your home to be a retreat. Understanding where both of you got your values from can then help you to decide what hospitality should look like for you. Then you can (hopefully) decide that you want a hospitable home but where you both take responsibility for guests and value each other.

## Read:

> [12] *You are always and dearly loved by God! So robe yourself with virtues of God, since you have been divinely chosen to be holy. Be merciful as you endeavor to understand others, and be compassionate, showing kindness toward all. Be gentle and humble, unoffendable in your patience with others.* [13] *Tolerate the weaknesses of those in the family of faith, forgiving one another in the same way you have been graciously forgiven by Jesus Christ. If you find fault with someone, release this same gift of forgiveness to them.* [14] *For love is supreme and must flow through each of these virtues. Love becomes the mark of true maturity.*

> COLOSSIANS 3 V 12-14 [TPT]

## Pray:

To be able to understand the values that you each have and to work towards shared values.

## Discuss:

Can you identify any mismatched values in your life together? If so, help each other to work out where they came from. What needs to change to accommodate both of your views and wishes?

You'll find more discussion points on the Values Tool Sheet in Appendix II on page 155.

## Declare:

I know my own values and hold the values of my partner as precious and important.

# GOING DEEPER

## DAY 8

# Time

When we work with couples we ask them to divide their time into four categories:

| A | Together time focussed on each other (e.g. date night, meal out or walk) |
|---|---|
| B | Together time but spent with others or together working jointly (a meal with friends, praying together or playing games) |
| C | Time spent close to each other , but not together (one making sandwiches, one bathing children), working separately |
| D | Time spent apart (at work or an unshared hobby) |

In a typical week we would suggest that for the sake of their relationship a couple should build the following into their personal schedules (a session being a morning/afternoon or evening):

| A | 1-2 sessions |
|---|---|
| B | 3- 4 sessions |
| C | 4- 8 sessions |
| D | The rest of the week |

However, it's not unusual to find that couples spend very little time with either "A" or "B" time but instead fill their lives with "C" and "D" and then wonder why their relationship is struggling!

GOING DEEPER

Use this grid to keep a track of how your days are spent;

| Day | Morning | Afternoon | Evening |
|---|---|---|---|
| For example. | D – at work | D – at work | C – Home Group |
| Monday | | | |
| Tuesday | | | |
| Wednesday | | | |
| Thursday | | | |
| Friday | | | |
| Saturday | | | |
| Sunday | | | |

Then review the last week, filling in the grid with your activity and type of time.

How do you do as a couple? Do you spend enough quality time together? Why not repeat the grid on page 33 in a couple of weeks time and see if things have changed?

| Day | Morning | Afternoon | Evening |
|---|---|---|---|
| For example. | D – at work | D – at work | C – Home Group |
| Monday | | | |
| Tuesday | | | |
| Wednesday | | | |
| Thursday | | | |
| Friday | | | |
| Saturday | | | |
| Sunday | | | |

## Read:

1. For everything there is a season,
   a time for every activity under heaven.
2. A time to be born and a time to die.
   A time to plant and a time to harvest.
3. A time to kill and a time to heal.
   A time to tear down and a time to build up.
4. A time to cry and a time to laugh.
   A time to grieve and a time to dance.
5. A time to scatter stones and a time to gather stones.
   A time to embrace and a time to turn away.
6. A time to search and a time to quit searching.
   A time to keep and a time to throw away.
7. A time to tear and a time to mend.
   A time to be quiet and a time to speak.
8. A time to love and a time to hate.

*A time for war and a time for peace.*

ECCLESIASTES 3 V 1–8 [NLT]

## Pray:

Spend some time praying about the distribution of your time you spent together or apart. Ask the Lord how and why you used your time in these ways. Are there ways that He wants you to change how you spend your time?

## Discuss:

How do you feel about this? Did you both allocate your week into the same categories? If not, then why the difference? What would more "A" time look like to you both?

## Declare:

Time is my tool and I will use it well for my relationship with my partner and others.

GOING DEEPER

DAY 9

# Arguing Well

It's healthy in a relationship to expect that there'll be some confrontation. What is not healthy is when confrontation becomes conflict, leading to a war where one of you 'wins' and the other has to 'lose'. If you never have a disagreement it can also mean that one or both of you don't care enough to fight any more!

Arguing should never be the goal, but healthy disagreement, or arguing well, can help deepen our knowledge and understanding of each other.

Here are some top tips for arguing well:-

- Call a truce – sometimes we can be so upset by 'the issue' that we need to call a truce to give one or both parties time to calm down. This needs to be agreed by both parties and not used as a weapon. If this is done then a time when conversation resumes should be mutually agreed.

- Agree a time to have your discussion – sometimes we get into disagreements at inappropriate moments, such as late at night or in front of others. We need be able to stop and mutually agree a more appropriate time to continue the conversation.

- Private not public – having an argument in front of others can cause humiliation and defensiveness that only adds to the issue. Choose to speak privately to each other. If you can resolve confrontation healthily then it can be helpful for your children to sometimes witness this so that they learn the skills to be able to argue well themselves.

## GOING DEEPER

- Re-affirm commitment – your partner is not your enemy and stopping to say, "I love you" and "I am committed to you" in a confrontation can diffuse rising emotions.

- Remember where you will be in an hour or days' time – this issue that seems so big now will often not be so important tomorrow. Remember that tomorrow you may well be back to normal and the issue resolved.

- Deal with the issue, not the person – blaming causes defensiveness, try instead to make statements about the issue that open up discussion. No one likes to be told they do this or that but most people will respond to, "When this happens I feel ….because…. and it would help if we could…"

- Be willing to listen – some people talk too much and need to learn to listen. Having the last word is not the most important thing. Working together to find a win-win solution should be the aim.

- Be willing to talk – the silent treatment can inflame a situation. If you need time to process what is being said, say so, don't just become silent.

- Be willing to be the first to say, "Sorry" – saying sorry and building bridges is more important than being right and losing your partner's trust. Saying "Sorry" and owning specific mistakes can create the bridge to being able to talk about the issue.

- Be prepared to forgive and forget – holding a grudge can kill a relationship. Learning to forgive each other clears the way for change to happen. Bringing up the past can create red hot buttons in the relationship.

- Don't press the 'red hot buttons'! We all have sensitive points, which, if thrown into a discussion by our partner, are likely to escalate the situation. Understand what these are and choose to avoid them in any confrontation. Knowing that if you say, "You are just like your mother!" will cause an explosion and using that tactic is not a clever way to win, it is manipulation which, Biblically, is akin to witchcraft.

- Be willing to get outside help – it is always better to ask for outside help that struggle on to the point of separation. We all need help from time to time.

Are there any of these you need to put into practice in your relationship? This is a good time to say sorry to your partner for the times you haven't treated them well in disagreements.

## Read:

> *"Above all, you must live as citizens of heaven, conducting yourselves in a manner worthy of the Good News about Christ. Then, whether I come and see you again or only hear about you, I will know that you are standing together with one Spirit and one purpose, fighting together for the faith, which is the Good News."*

PHILIPPIANS 1 V 28[NLT]

## Pray:

Take some time to say sorry to God for the times you have not responded well in conflict and have wounded your partner.

## Discuss:

Are there ways you could improve how you sort things out when there's a problem? Is there anything either of you does that exacerbates a row rather than helping to settle it?

## Declare:

I thank you Lord that You confront me with my need to change, I am open to being changed.

GOING DEEPER

**DAY 10**

# Resolving Issues

Is it possible to resolve issues in a relationship? The answer is 'Yes', but it may not be the most important thing! Sometimes our reason for wanting to resolve issues is just so that we can win an argument, however more important than winning is the connection we have with our partner. Winning can sometimes break the connection, more important than winning is understanding and being understood. We don't always want our partner to do what we say, but we do want them to understand why we find something an issue, we want to have connection with them.

If a couple seeks to understand each other and work together to build connection, even when they disagree, they will actually be able to have unresolved issues in their marriage and still enjoy a happy marriage. This might seem counter-intuitive but it is actually true. John Gottam, a psychology professor who researched couples for more than 40 years, found that even happy couples can have unresolved issues, but that they had maintained connection and deepened understanding of one another rather than letting these issues drive a wedge between them.[1]

The next time you disagree stop yourself from getting defensive and ask, "What is going on for my partner right now, what do I need to understand about them or this issue that I am not understanding?"

A key characteristic to living with unresolved issue is humility. Humility is not thinking less of yourself, it is thinking about yourself less (often). With real humility we can be less concerned about being understood and more concerned about understanding.

[1] John Gottam *The Seven Principles for Making Marriage Work* Harmony Books 2015

## Read:

1     *Is there any encouragement from belonging to Christ? Any comfort from his love? Any fellowship together in the Spirit? Are your hearts tender and compassionate?*

2     *Then make me truly happy by agreeing wholeheartedly with each other, loving one another, and working together with one mind and purpose.*

3     *Don't be selfish; don't try to impress others. Be humble, thinking of others as better than yourselves. ⁴ Don't look out only for your own interests, but take an interest in others, too.*

5     *You must have the same attitude that Christ Jesus had.*

6     *Though he was God he did not think of equality with God as something to cling to.*

7     *Instead, he gave up his divine privileges; he took the humble position of a slave*
     *and was born as a human being. When he appeared in human form,*

8     *he humbled himself in obedience to God and died a criminal's death on a cross.*

9     *Therefore, God elevated him to the place of highest honor and gave him the name above all other names,*

10     *that at the name of Jesus every knee should bow, in heaven and on earth and under the earth,*

11     *and every tongue declare that Jesus Christ is Lord, to the glory of God the Father.*

PHILIPPIANS 2 V 1-11 [NLT]

## Pray:

Think about the connection you have with your partner and pray about how this can be deepened. Pray for humility to be a trade mark of your relationship together.

## Discuss:

How do you both feel when you disagree? Do you get defensive? Do you attack? Is there a way that you can agree to always look for a "win-win" resolution when you fall out with each other?

## Declare:

My opinions matter but so do other people's. I will love like the Lord who knows all of me and still chooses to love me.

GOING DEEPER

GOING DEEPER

DAY 11

# Understanding Repair Attempts

John Gottam, in *"The Seven Principles for Making Marriage Work"*[2] talks about repair attempts. These are the moments when we are disagreeing with each other and one of us tries to say something to diffuse the situation. It could be that Mary says to John, "You never clear up in the kitchen." John then replies, "Don't you remember last week when I made a meal for us and tided up?" Mary can take this as John being defensive or she can see it as him making a repair attempt. How Mary responds is crucial to whether this becomes a disagreement or is diffused. If Mary agrees with John and chooses to remember the times he has cleaned up, then a new way is made possible. Mary and John could then discuss why Mary feels that John is not doing his fair share and, rather than arguing, agree a way forward together. If Mary continues to accuse John the outcome is likely to be very different – possibly more mess being made with more tidying up to be done!

Do you recognise the times when your partner has tried to make a repair attempt in your relationship? Those moments in a disagreement when they become conciliatory, reminding you of something which will help if you let it or even make you smile? Finding ways to make repair attempts and recognising repair attempts can be a way to move disagreements from the place where they lead to conflict to a place where your relationship can move forward.

It would seem this is a very Biblical thing to do. Remember the story in Acts 15 where two groups of Christians had very different views on how to let Gentiles be Christians? Should they have to take on all the Jewish laws or not?

[2] John Gottam *The Seven Principles for Making Marriage Work* Harmony Books 2015

43

GOING DEEPER

## Read:

> 6 So the apostles and elders met together to resolve this issue. 7 At the meeting, after a long discussion, Peter stood and addressed them as follows: "Brothers, you all know that God chose me from among you some time ago to preach to the Gentiles so that they could hear the Good News and believe. 8 God knows people's hearts, and he confirmed that he accepts Gentiles by giving them the Holy Spirit, just as he did to us. 9 He made no distinction between us and them, for he cleansed their hearts through faith. 10 So why are you now challenging God by burdening the Gentile believers with a yoke that neither we nor our ancestors were able to bear? 11 We believe that we are all saved the same way, by the undeserved grace of the Lord Jesus.
>
> 12 Everyone listened quietly as Barnabas and Paul told about the miraculous signs and wonders God had done through them among the Gentiles."
>
> ACTS 15 V 6-12 NLT

What Peter did was a huge repair attempt. Instead of arguing, he presented a repair attempt by telling the testimony of what God was doing among the Gentiles. The rest of the apostles and elders could have gone back to arguing scripture, instead they listen and respond to this 'repair attempt' by finding a new way to incorporate Gentile believers.

If it's possible with a group of people then surely it should be so much more with our spouse! Why not give it a go? Learn to spot those repair attempts in your relationship.

## Pray:

Write a declaration together that you keep speaking over your relationship: determine that you'll both learn to spot these repair attempts and accept them and then work through your differences

## Discuss:

Having just written your joint declaration, how do you feel? Have you noticed your spouse make any repair attempts? Have you?

## Declare:

Read aloud the declaration you have just written.

GOING DEEPER

GOING DEEPER

**DAY 12**

# The Enemy Within:
# Confrontation and Conflict

Forgive us being slightly tongue in cheek when we say that we're sure that no-one reading this will ever have experienced conflict in their marriage. After all, we're all Christians, aren't we, and we don't do that kind of thing. At least, not in public. Of course it's quite possible that this is entirely true, and the two of you are in serene love with each other, in which case consider today a holiday whilst the rest of us try and get to where you already are!

What's important in a marriage is not that you argue but that you resolve your arguments well, and what can make all the difference is your understanding of the difference between confrontation and conflict. Confrontation is a fairly normal part of everyday married life. One of you wants or needs something not being given to you by the other. It can be as simple as not putting the milk back in the fridge after using it. If you're both prepared to talk about this openly the matter can be resolved easily. "Darling, I wish you'd put the milk back in the fridge when you're finished with it." "Whoops, I'm so sorry, I'll make sure I do so in future." Two short sentences and the whole confrontation is resolved. You've both recognised that your marriage isn't a contest, there's no winner and loser. You both have to be winners, practically and emotionally.

Now try this: "Darling, I wish you'd put the milk back in the fridge when you're finished with it." "Put it in the fridge yourself, I'm busy." Suddenly one of you is the loser. Notice that there's no blame, no accusation, there doesn't have to be, there's a lack of love and an unspoken rejection and that's all it takes. This couple are in conflict because, on the face of it, one of them either has to be a doormat or fight back.

Here's the point. It takes strength and character to be on the receiving end of unkindness and be neither a doormat or fight back, and it's a choice one has to make. What's the choice? It's to turn towards your partner without being defensive and aim to resolve the problem rather than let it escalate.

How does that work? How can they recover? It's going to take both of them to want to and to be prepared to be understanding with each other. It will take an expression of remorse and sorrow for having caused pain. It will take being willing to listen, understand and forgive. But most of all it takes that first step of turning towards your partner without rancour or hurt.

Here are some further top tips:

- Always deal with the issue, not the person.

- Don't accuse, "I feel" is a lot more helpful than an accusing "You…".

- Be ready to say you're sorry, and mean it.

- Be ready to forgive and forget!

And be ready to get third party help if your confrontations continually slip in to conflict. Your relationship is important!

## Read:

*You are always and dearly loved by God! So robe yourself with virtues of God, since you have been divinely chosen to be holy. Be merciful as you endeavor to understand others, and be compassionate, showing kindness toward all. Be gentle and humble, unoffendable in your patience with others. 13 Tolerate the weaknesses of those in the family of faith, forgiving one another in the same way you have been graciously forgiven by Jesus Christ. If you find fault with someone, release this same gift of forgiveness to them. 14 For love is supreme and must flow through each of these virtues. Love becomes the mark of true maturity.*

COLOSSIANS 3 V 12- 14 [TPT]

## Pray:

Father God help me to be choose to resolve arguments with my spouse and to react in love even when I feel under attack.

## Discuss:

How you can help each other to react well in disagreements. Think of some times when using "I" statements would help. What would you say instead of accusing?

## Declaration:

I choose to resolve issues with my partner and not accuse them.

GOING DEEPER

## DAY 13

# Love Languages

Some years ago Gary Chapman wrote a helpful book called 'The Five Love Languages'[1]. In it he identified these love languages as being one way of looking at how we give and receive love. The five love languages he identified are:-

1.  Quality time - not just spending time with someone but really focusing on that person. It is not about what we do but the fact we are choosing to be with them.

2.  Touch - physical touch, not talking about sex here, but touch, such as a hand on my arm as you talk to me, a hug, holding hands or a hair rub.

3.  Gifts - it doesn't have to be a big thing, it can be a little present that means such a lot, especially if it's been thought through and beautifully wrapped!

4.  Acts of service - this is any practical way I can serve you from making a cup of tea, to doing jobs around the house.

5.  Words of affirmation. Verbally expressing your affection and appreciation of your partner.

Learning each other's love languages is not just about understanding how we each give and receive love to and from one another but also how we can hurt each other with a love language. For example if my love language is physical touch – I will feel loved when you hug me, put an arm round or hold my hand, but if you withhold physical touch, that can feel like a punishment.

[1] Gary Chapman *Five Love languages* Moody Publishers 2015

Understanding this can be really important in making our partner feel loved in those moments of difficulty or during stressful times. A word of affirmation in a stressful moment can say "I love you" but it can also reassure.

If you're not sure of your love language there is an online test that you can take at www.5lovelanguages.com/quizzes/. Once you know each other's love languages it can be helpful to discuss not just the ways in which you can positively love each other in that language but also where you should not punish each other by withdrawal of it.

It might be (like lots of marriages) you have completely opposite love languages – this exercise is even more important for you as learning to love your partner in their love language can build a deep connection between you both.

## Read:

7 *Dear friends, I am not writing a new commandment for you; rather it is an old one you have had from the very beginning. This old commandment—to love one another—is the same message you heard before.* 8 *Yet it is also new. Jesus lived the truth of this commandment, and you also are living it. For the darkness is disappearing, and the true light is already shining.*

9 *If anyone claims, 'I am living in the light,' but hates a fellow believer, that person is still living in darkness. Anyone who loves a fellow believer is living in the light and does not cause others to stumble.*

1 JOHN 2 V 7-10 NLT

## Pray:

Ask for God to fill you up with His love so that you can love your partner well in the way that they receive it.

## Discuss:

If you haven't before, do you know each other's love languages? If so, do you feel that your spouse honours yours? How could they do more? How could you?

## Declare:

Lord you know me completely and love me utterly. I commit to new ways of understanding myself and my spouse.

GOING DEEPER

DAY 14

# Friendship

C.S. Lewis said, "The most precious gift that marriage gave me was the constant impact of something very close and intimate, yet all the time unmistakably other, resistant - in a word, real"[1]. We all want that deep connection with another person, and one of the ways we get this is by having a friendship with our partner.

Do you expect that your partner will be your best friend? Some couples want this to be the case, some couples haven't even thought about it. In a world where lust and chemistry is often seen as the most important thing to bring a couple together, then friendship can be something that we bypass. However, if we want a long-lasting relationship then friendship is the best foundation for a good marriage. Lust will come and go, how we are attracted to each other may need to change but friendship can develop to sustain us through all of this.

Think about those things that first attracted you to your partner, there will be of course be physical attraction but hopefully in that list are some qualities that you would seek in a good friend. What are those qualities? Have you ever told your partner that you value those qualities too?

What are the qualities of friendship that we want to enjoy in a marriage? Loyalty, openness, sharing, being there in times of need, providing support, honesty, mutual understanding, kindness and compassion are all things that can be found in friendships. They also make great qualities to have in a marriage!

Jesus chooses to call us His friends - so actually being a friend is a high calling! Why would we not want to be this for our partner? How do you foster friendship between you? Good communication is key, shared

[1] C.S. Lewis *A Grief Observed* Faber and Faber 2013

interests, spending time together and keeping on growing in mutual understanding all also help.

Having our spouse as our best friend doesn't mean we can't have other friends. Both men and women need to have other friendships to enrich their lives, but having your spouse as your best friend is a blessings for life.

## Read:

[1] *After David had finished talking with Saul, he met Jonathan, the king's son. There was an immediate bond between them, for Jonathan loved David. [2] From that day on Saul kept David with him and wouldn't let him return home. [3] And Jonathan made a solemn pact with David, because he loved him as he loved himself. [4] Jonathan sealed the pact by taking off his robe and giving it to David, together with his tunic, sword, bow, and belt*

I SAMUEL 18 V 1– 4 [NLT]

## Pray:

Talk to God about how you can deepen the friendship between you.

## Discuss:

Have you ever talked about your friendship with each other and what it means to you? Or could you be closer and better friends? If so, what would it take?

## Declare:

Friendship is a privilege with You, Lord. I will build friendship with my partner.

GOING DEEPER

DAY 15

# Boundaries, Day 1

You might wonder why a potentially divisive subject such as boundaries is included in a devotional for couples. Surely the last thing one wants to see between a man and his wife, a wife and her husband are boundaries! Well, you're both right and wrong, it depends on what you mean by the word 'boundaries'.

Let's start with what the opposite of a boundary could be. One could think of a boundary as a wall, protecting what's inside it from being seen or entered by all that's outside. If that's the case then the opposite is going to be boundaryless and may best be described as 'nothing hidden'. And that's exactly the way things should be in marriage, a relationship in which nothing is hidden from each other, where truth prevails and in which nothing is ever so threatening to the relationship that is cannot be shared.

There are others boundaries though, and these you do want. These are the boundaries that protect both your relationship and your marriage, boundaries that keep you safe. Danny Silk in his book "Keep Your Love On" teaches on boundaries. He points out that to protect our relationships we need to establish healthy priorities and boundaries around both ourselves and the level on intimacy we nurture with each person. Let's look at that. Danny sometimes illustrates his talks on boundaries by drawing a series of circles around a dot, that dot representing you. Now, he asks, who do you allow into that inner circle and into each of the circles that radiate out from you. In the innermost circle your spouse, certainly, children, yes, your siblings, probably. Your parents? Again probably, but how will your spouse feel about this, and come to that, about your siblings? And how about close friends and your business partner?

Here's the thing, that boundary is there to protect you and you only allow those very closest to you into that inner sanctum. It's a healthy thing to have. If you're in our inner circle our door is always open to you. If you're in the next circle out, you have my number, ring and make an appointment. If you're in the next circle out again then ring my secretary or email me to make an appointment. And the busier you are as a person, the more boundary circles you'll have; there'll always be movement between the circles too, as some people become closer for a season, and others drift out of your life. These boundaries are important for those most precious to you. It's how you protect your relationship with them.

## Read:

*Once again Jesus withdrew with his disciples to the lakeside, but a massive crowd of people followed him from all around the provinces of Galilee and southern Israel.*

MARK 3 V 7 [TPT]

Jesus withdrew, sometimes to be alone, sometimes to be with his disciples. If Jesus needed to do this to maintain the relationships he had, how much more important is it that we do too.

## Discuss:

What boundaries do I have or not? Has my lack of boundaries been affecting my marriage? How can we make changes?

## Pray:

Ask Father God to help you with changes you need to make to have healthy boundaries in your marriage.

## Declaration:

I will make healthy boundaries, I choose to understand that in saying "No" to some things I am saying "Yes" to my marriage

GOING DEEPER

GOING DEEPER

DAY 16

# Boundaries, Day 2

We spoke yesterday about boundaries and how these can be both good and bad, depending on your understanding of the word. We decided that any boundary between you and your spouse was a bad thing, but that it was wise to have social boundaries to protect you and your inner circle of family and close friends from those people who decide for themselves that they want to get close to you.

There is an additional important point to make here, there should only be one other person who should be able to dictate your boundaries and that's your spouse. It is only too easy, especially if you are an extravert who loves people, to be happy to allow all and sundry into your life with no thought to a boundary, whilst your introvert spouse wants nothing more that peace and quiet and you to themselves. Somewhere in this a compromise that is acceptable to you both has to be found and laid down.

There's one other application for the word 'boundary,' and we alluded to it in the quote by Danny Silk yesterday. What he said is that we all need to establish healthy priorities and boundaries around both ourselves and the level of intimacy we nurture with each person.

Let's look at the second part of the last sentence; to nurture is to feed and encourage, and Danny's use of the word is particularly meaningful. We can be with someone and work and play and be a best friend to them for years without ever feeling the need to feed or encourage or somehow take the relationship to a different level or place.

Aren't the best friendships, after all, those where you know exactly where you stand with each other without having to talk about it. Sometimes though, sometimes, especially if it's a friend of the opposite sex, there awakes one day that urge to make something more than it is…and that's what Danny is warning us about, because if that urge is given in to we'll be "nurturing the level of intimacy we have with that person", and that's a boundary we should never cross.

## Read:

> *Repay no one evil for evil, but give thought to do what is honourable in the sight of all. If possible, so far as it depends on you, live peaceably with all.*
>
> ROMANS 12 V 17-18 ESV

## Pray:

Father God show me any relationships where I have not got a healthy boundary and how to put that boundary in place for the sake of my marriage.

## Discuss:

The different relationships you have and any that may need readjusting in light of today's subject.

## Declaration:

My marriage is the most important relationship and I choose to forsake all others in order to nurture this relationship

GOING DEEPER

DAY 17

# Expectations

Having expectations can be both good and bad and that's what we'll be looking at today. First, though, a question: would you say that you live your life with a glass that's half full or one that's half empty, because the answer to this question will probably determine whether for you having and living with expectations is a good or bad thing. Here's a hint: having a constant optimism about the future, your glass half full, must be a good thing, and always expecting the worst…well, who'd want to live like that if they didn't have to?

There's another side to this conversation, though. Optimism and having expectation of good things is fine, but not when we start to place our expectations, good or bad, on other people, especially our spouses. Now, here's the point we want to make. We shouldn't need to depend on the expectations we've placed on other people, spouses included, to make us feel happy and complete, and the word here is "depend". There a world of difference between looking forward to something happening that will bless you and others involved, and placing expectations on people or events that, if they don't happen, turns your world upside down. One is a "glass half full" attitude towards life, the other is "glass half empty". One is living life as a contributor, the other is living it as a dependent.

Let's explore this a little further. If there's one thing that will unbalance the equilibrium of a happy marriage it's an unequal dependency between wife and husband. Now, don't hear us wrong on this. Yes, there's something loving and sweet about a mutual dependence on each other being the bedrock of the relationship, but 'mutual' in this case means 'equal'. When one in the relationship demands more from the other than they give the 'mutual equality' in the relationship receives two blows at once. Whoever is doing the demanding is suddenly giving less, and their spouse ends up receiving less and having to give more out of this less. Does that make sense? It usually doesn't take long for the resentment that this inequality fosters to rise to the surface.

## Read:

> [8] *Now, this is the goal: to live in harmony with one another and demonstrate affectionate love, sympathy, and kindness toward other believers. Let humility describe who you are as you dearly love one another.* [9] *Never retaliate when someone treats you wrongly, nor insult those who insult you, but instead, respond by speaking a blessing over them—because a blessing is what God promised to give you.*
>
> PETER 3 V 8–9 [TPT]

## Pray:

Father God, help us both to live a life that's always "glass half full", a life of humility and love for one another.

## Discuss:

What expectations do you feel you have of your partner? Do you feel they are met or crushed? What can you do to have a more equal relationship.

## Declaration:

We declare that we will not have unreasonable expectations on each other

GOING DEEPER

DAY 18

# Sex Life

It might seem a little strange to include a day on sex in a devotional book for married couples but it's not. Sex is one of God's many great ideas! The sexual act was one God created to be part of marriage and to solidify the connection between man and woman. Ephesians likens the act of sexual intimacy to the mystery of the union between Christ and the church. Sex is not just a physical act, it has a spiritual significance in our marriage in the way it bonds us together.

There is a perception that sex is something we do a lot until children arrive, then it becomes something the man wants but the woman doesn't until eventually we stop having it altogether. It doesn't have to be like this, sex can be a precious part of life together, bringing closeness throughout married life into and through our old age. We might have to get creative as our bodies change and adapt to their differing needs but there is no reason why it should be something we stop doing.

Do you talk about sex with your spouse? Your own thoughts and needs for sex changes over time and so will your partner's, so you shouldn't presume you know how your partner feels about things. Our bodies change over time, women's bodies not only have to cope with the challenges of monthly cycles but pregnancy and menopause bring their own unique challenges. We'd be naive to say that men's bodies don't undergo changes too! Whatever you think about the male menopause, we all grow older!

Other things like job loss, bereavement, children and changes in career can affect our libido. Without talking about these things our partner might feel we are rejecting them when actually we are just coping with change.

Of course our past history can affect our sex life too – experience of abuse, rape or body trauma can have a dramatic impact on our ability or willingness to be intimate. A promiscuous past can bring additional challenges. None of these things are insurmountable but we do have to talk to each other and seek healing from whatever the past has brought with it. Often bringing understanding lowers stress and creates the platform to having a fulfilling and fulfilled sex life.

The key, then, to a good sex life is to keep talking to each other, to overcome the embarrassment, know what you both enjoy or don't, to honour each other and learn to fulfil each other's needs in a way that builds you both up.

# Read:

> [3] *The husband should fulfil his wife's sexual needs, and the wife should fulfil her husband's needs.* [4] *The wife gives authority over her body to her husband, and the husband gives authority over his body to his wife.*
>
> [5] *Do not deprive each other of sexual relations, unless you both agree to refrain from sexual intimacy for a limited time so you can give yourselves more completely to prayer. Afterward, you should come together again so that Satan won't be able to tempt you because of your lack of self-control.*
>
> 1 CORINTHIANS 7 V 3-5 [NLT]

## Pray:

Pray about the sexual side of your relationship, ask God how you can honour each other in your sexual life together.

## Discuss:

How easy do you find it to talk about sex? Did your parents? How did them doing, or not doing, so influence you? Would you like to be able to be more open with each other?

## Declare:

Sex is a good gift from God for me and my partner. We communicate well and strengthen our sex life.

GOING DEEPER

GOING DEEPER

DAY 19

# Soul Ties

What is a soul tie? It's the bond we are meant to have in relationships. We can have soul ties in any relationship, for example with our partner or with children and friends. These soul ties are meant to be the healthy connections we have with people. Unfortunately, they can be unhealthy or we can have lasting soul ties to old partners that can affect current relationships.

Relationships develop – so a healthy soul tie with a child when they are young will look like me helping them learn to feed, use the toilet, and do other basic skills. However, if I am still telling my 20 year old son to use the toilet there is something wrong! This soul tie has become unhealthy because it's holding both of us in out of date patterns of thought and behaviour. Soul ties have a natural shelf life and in our relationship with our spouse we need to make sure that we have dealt with old soul ties so that they don't affect our life together. If we still dream or think about an old girlfriend or boyfriend then there is probably a soul tie that we need to cut off. There can also be other unhealthy soul ties we need to deal with for our marriage to thrive. For example, if we have an unhealthy soul tie with a parent or friend that limits or compromises our connection with our partner, then we need to deal with it. If my first reaction is to talk to a friend or parent, rather than my spouse, then this can show that I am connected in the wrong way, I have an unhealthy soul tie.

Dealing with a soul tie is not a complicated process, we just need to pray it through, asking God to break all unhealthy soul ties with that person If you don't believe that soul ties have power, look at this passage from Corinthians. Under the New Testament covenant the believing wife brings holiness into her marriage through the soul tie she has with her unbelieving partner.

## Read:

12   *Now, I will speak to the rest of you, though I do not have a direct command from the Lord. If a fellow believer has a wife who is not a believer and she is willing to continue living with him, he must not leave her.* 13 *And if a believing woman has a husband who is not a believer and he is willing to continue living with her, she must not leave him.* 14 *For the believing wife brings holiness to her marriage, and the believing husband brings holiness to his marriage. Otherwise, your children would not be holy, but now they are holy.* 15 *But if the husband or wife who isn't a believer insists on leaving, let them go. In such cases the believing husband or wife is no longer bound to the other, for God has called you to live in peace.* 16 *Don't you wives realize that your husbands might be saved because of you? And don't you husbands realize that your wives might be saved because of you?*

I CORINTHIANS 7 V12- 16 NLT

## Pray:

Ask God to show you if you have any soul ties that need breaking.

Then pray this for each person:-

Jesus, I break any unhealthy soul ties with ...............................
And I send back to them all the negative effects of that relationship and I take back anything that was taken from me within that relationship and I restore it to myself, washed in the blood of Jesus.

## Discuss:

Have you ever suspected or thought that your spouse may have a historic soul-tie? How does this make you feel? What would you both like to do about it?

## Declare:

I live with healthy soul ties in my relationships.

GOING DEEPER

GOING DEEPER

DAY 20

# Dealing with Parents and In-laws

In jokes, mothers-in-laws often get an unfair battering but the reality is that relationships with our in-laws can be challenging. Often parents struggle to let go of their son or daughter to a new person or they can want to continue to influence the new family to do things their way.

This is why the Bible talks about leaving and cleaving – we leave our parents, the family we have been part of and form a new unit, a new family. You'll remember that we touched on this in Day 2. However, it's worth exploring this a bit further. Many couples struggle with how to do this in a way that honours and maintains good relationship with both sets of parents. The aim is to create and cleave to this new family unit, choosing for yourselves new ways of being and doing what you want together and the values you choose to have.

It sounds easy – leave and cleave, but the reality is that we often come into our marriage not being fully aware of the assumptions and expectations we have because of the family we grew up in. It's a good idea to take some time and ask some questions about this. What were the things we liked in our childhood home? What were the things we didn't like and want to change going forward? Finding out what our partner feels about their childhood home is helpful. This then opens up the possibility of a discussion around what elements of our pasts we would like to keep in this new family unit.

If you are just starting your married life you can decide from the beginning how you both want to deal with your in-laws and parents. Many of us will have been married for many years and already got some unhealthy habits. Don't worry it's not too late to make changes.

Of course, the challenge can then be in communicating to one's parents the way your unit has chosen to do something, especially when it clashes with the way that it has been done in their home. It is so important to do this in a loving and honouring way, without being critical of what the parents did.

It's also important to remember that we are not responsible for how our parents react to what we tell them – be that well or with offense. Our responsibility is for the way we communicate and relate to our parents.

In this process it's good to make sure we deal with any hurts our parents may have caused us that we're still holding on to. If we hold onto hurt, we are more likely to throw out the good with the bad. The aim for each family unit should be that when we release our children into a new family unit that our ceiling becomes their floor, so that they build on what we have learnt and understood.

Good communication with parents and in-laws can save a lot of hurt. We have to remember our being married is a change for them too, one they may not have been through before, unless we have older siblings. If we can talk to parents and navigate these changes well, then it's good for everyone. We can also help our spouse navigate what it means to relate to our own parents. Every family has their own culture and so much misunderstanding can come from not understanding the in-law's culture. Liz remembers that when she first met Stuart's parents she declared that cricket was a boring game, not understanding that the family loved cricket and that the TV was on because they all liked it, even although no-one seemed to be watching. That would have been a helpful thing to know beforehand and could have saved a lot of misunderstanding!

## Read:

*Honor your father and mother. Then you will live a long, full life in the land the LORD your God is giving you*

EXODUS 20 V 12 [NLT]

## Pray:

Thank God for your parents and the good things that they have passed on to you. Pray for healthy relationships with your in-laws.

## Discuss:

If you're newly-weds this may be a good time to be open about your feelings about each other's parents and to mutually work through how to get over any misgivings. If you've been married for some time a better discussion may be how you can rectify any remaining misunderstandings or problems.

## Declare:

I will learn from both my own family's culture and that of my partner's to build a Kingdom foundation for my marriage.

GOING DEEPER

GOING DEEPER

DAY 21

# The Child Effect

Children are a gift from God but that doesn't mean that everything that happens when we have children is easy to cope with or a blessing! Even the choice over when, or if, to have children can be a challenge for some. If we make it to the place where we get pregnant and children happen, we have to be prepared for the fact that whilst they can bring much joy they also bring changes to our relationship.

Not only does a woman's body go through major change during and after having children, the physical reality of a child changes the dynamics of a marriage. Suddenly this unit that was just about two people becomes about three people, or more. Time that we had for each other has to be shared with these little people, little people that can wake early in the morning and continue wide awake all day, exhausting us until we collapse in the evening. Then they wake us, frequently, during the night!

Thinking in advance about how we want to bring up our children and cope with the changes they cause is the ideal way to begin the process but if we haven't done that, and we already have children, it's never too late to think about the impact our children are having on our marriage. Some things we may want to consider are;

- What are the core values we want to impart to our children?
- How do we feel about discipline?
- What are the key ways we want to communicate love to our child?
- How do we want to balance time with our child and each other? What family traditions do we want to create?

Children are a blessing and can add to our marriage, but we do have to find ways to spend time with each other and still prioritise each other. Secure children grow up in marriages that are thriving, so we bless our

79

children if we keep investing in our marriage.

One thing that happens when you have children is that people start to tell you about how exhausting babies are, the terrible twos, the tantruming threes, the challenges of school age kids and, boy oh boy, don't get people started on the 'joys' of teenagers. You can listen to this narrative and take it on board and see every phase of childhood as one that has to be endured or suffered. Or you can choose to not listen to these prophets of doom and see each new phase of your children's development as one that will bring many joys. This way you get to enjoy what each phase brings rather than entering each with dread!

Proverbs tells us there is the power of life and death in the tongue (Proverbs 18 v 21). Be careful what you speak out over your children, because if you tell then, even jokingly, that they are little monsters, don't be surprised if that's what you reap. Learn to praise your children for the blessing that they are. Aim to 'pull out the gold' in them with encouraging words and by honouring them when they seek to invest in relationships with you and others.

Remember that you don't have to do this parenting on your own, not only can you be a support and encouragement to each other, you also have the Holy Spirit. He is our teacher and He is also a great parent! Even if you don't know what to do, you are connected to someone who does and, guess what, He is willing to share those secrets with you! Spending time with Holy Spirit when you are not sure how to parent and involving Him in the process can bring wisdom and insight we do not have on our own.

# Read:

*Unless the LORD builds a house,*
*the work of the builders is wasted.*
*Unless the LORD protects a city,*
*guarding it with sentries will do no good.*
*It is useless for you to work so hard*
*from early morning until late at night,*
*anxiously working for food to eat;*
*for God gives rest to his loved ones.*
*Children are a gift from the LORD;*
*they are a reward from him.*
*Children born to a young man*
*are like arrows in a warrior's hands.*
*How joyful is the man whose quiver is full of them!*
*He will not be put to shame when he confronts his accusers*
*at the city gates.*

PSALM 127 NLT

# Pray:

If you have children then pray for each of them and your relationship with them. Pray for your marriage and ways you can grow your marriage so that your children are secure.

# Discuss:

Again, if you have children, when did you last sit and talk about your hopes and aspirations for them with each other? And if you haven't, how do you both feel about that? It's always good to catch up with each other's feelings!

# Declare:

Children, in all their stages of development, are a blessing. My marriage will be ideal ground in which to prosper.

GOING DEEPER

GOING DEEPER

**DAY 22**

# Worship

Worship is not just about the songs we sing or going to church together but the whole of our lives and how we live them for God. Let's take today to look at how we can encourage a life of worship together. It would be easy to think that if you are both musical or worship leaders that this would be easier to do, but since worship is about our heart position to God, and not how beautiful our singing is, then creating an atmosphere of worship in our home is something we can all attain to.

Worship begins with turning our affection towards God in the morning and, if we have asked Holy Spirit to keep connecting with our spirit, continues through to nightfall as we sleep. Worship in marriage is about choosing, together, to turn our affections, our hearts, towards God. Worship in marriage is about creating a culture that makes it easy for our partner and our children to 'tune in' to God.

How do we do that? Learning to spend time in contemplative and sung worship together is a good start; putting on some good worship music and joining together to sing and speak out our praises are good things to do. Also, letting our worship flow from us in the moments we face difficulties will deepen our ongoing connection to the Lord.

> *Happy are those who hear the joyful call to worship,*
> *for they will walk in the light of your presence, LORD.*

PSALM 89 V 15 NLT

It may be that one of you likes words and so you like to write your own Psalms or speak out words of praise and worship. For the other, it may be sung praise that helps you worship. Learning to understand what brings each other into the presence of God is important for having a worship life together.

A worshipful attitude so that even in the midst of challenges you join together to praise God, in whatever way you like to do so, can create a different atmosphere around you. It's not always easy to make that choice when it feels like a situation is going from bad to worse but it really does make a difference.

## Read:

*But the hour is coming, and is now here, when the true worshipers will worship the Father in spirit and truth, for the Father is seeking such people to worship him.*

JOHN 4 V 23 ESV

*And Jesus answered him, And Jesus answered him, "It is written, 'You shall worship the Lord your God, and him only shall you serve.'".*

LUKE 4 V 8 ESV

*Therefore let us be grateful for receiving a kingdom that cannot be shaken, and thus let us offer to God acceptable worship, with reverence and awe,*

HEBREWS 12 V 28 ESV

## Pray:

Spend some time together worshipping God – you can do this through sung and said praise.

## Discuss:

It may be that today's topic highlights a way of worshipping that you're not used to. It may even feel uncomfortable. Can you see the value of worshipping in this way? How could you start to introduce daily worship into your lives?

## Declare:

I fix my life to thankfulness and praise. I declare with thought, words and action Your greatness and goodness, O Lord.

GOING DEEPER

GOING DEEPER

**DAY 23**

# Spiritual Life – A Three Stranded Cord

*Three are even better, for a triple-braided cord is not easily broken.*

ECCLESIASTES 4 V12 [NLT]

We have all probably sat in weddings where this verse has been quoted and nodded in agreement that a triple braided cord is not easily broken. We want God to be at the centre of our marriage, but how do we achieve this? Our own Spiritual lives are unique to us and can be very different, so how do we learn to have one together?

Our joint Spiritual life begins with each partner having a Spiritual life of their own. This might seem like Spiritual life 101, but you would be amazed at how many Christians never pick up the Bible or pray on their own, which makes it very unlikely they will pray together! Develop your own secret history with God and you will find this will inevitably spill into your history together. If your individual response is to pray about things, worship God in every situation and pick up the Bible for wisdom and insight, then you are more likely to do this together.

"When I have learned to love God better than my earthly dearest, I shall love my earthly dearest better than I do now." CS Lewis.[1]. The reality is that when we have a deeper connection with God it helps us to love our partner better too!

When you have taken this first step of developing your own Spiritual life then you will find that it will overflow into your time together. After

[1] C.S. Lewis *Letters of C.S. Lewis* 8 November, 1952

GOING DEEPER

that you can encourage your Spiritual life together. Work out when would be a good time to pray together in your day and aim to do that as a regular practice. While we would all like to think that we can do this for a good chunk of time, even praying for five minutes each day is better than never doing it.

Find ways to read the Bible together, whether this is sharing from what you have read individually or working through a Bible passage together, it doesn't matter. The purpose of sharing God's word together is to hear God's heart for your marriage.

More important even than the Spiritual disciplines of prayer, worship and Bible reading is that together you put God at the centre of your marriage. This is about more than praying together, but will be worked out in the values you have, the purpose of your marriage, what priorities you have, how you spend time and money, and how you raise your children. Coming together in each area, asking God what His plans are and putting Him at the centre of your decision-making process is key to becoming a three stranded cord.

## Read:

*Two people are better off than one, for they can help each other succeed. If one person falls, the other can reach out and help. But someone who falls alone is in real trouble. Likewise, two people lying close together can keep each other warm. But how can one be warm alone? A person standing alone can be attacked and defeated, but two can stand back-to-back and conquer. Three are even better, for a triple-braided cord is not easily broken.*

ECCLESIASTES 4 V 9-12 NLT

## Pray:

Spend some time praying through how God can be at the centre of your life together. Think about the different areas of your life (work, finances, church, family) and ask Him how you can keep Him at the centre.

## Discuss:

Today, talk with each other about how you can encourage your Spiritual life together. Is there anything in this you would find uncomfortable? How will you get over this?

## Declare:

Every day I take new steps to live from a deep and real spiritual life. I do this for the glory of God and to invest in the spiritual life of my marriage.

GOING DEEPER

GOING DEEPER

DAY 24

# Dealing with Differences

Very few people like everything about their partner. From irritating habits to differences in opinions, desires, hobbies and plans we are different from each other and some of those differences can be challenging! Most of us can smile at the differences that don't matter too much, like preferring different foods or odd choice of TV programmes. The differences that are harder to deal with are when we come to the bigger issues like having children or the plans we want to make for the future. We have to face the reality that we are two different people, with two different personalities, two past histories and two sets of opinions. The more we understand these differences and why they are there, the easier we will find it to navigate through them. If our partner comes out with an opinion we don't like our reaction to this will depend on how much understanding we have of them and why they're saying what they are. Taking time to find out about our partner, what personality type they are, what influenced them in their upbringing, what dreams and plans they have will help us appreciate them.

It also helps if we understand ourselves too. Many people don't know much about their own personality or how their history has shaped them. Discovering these things can help our partner get to know us better but may also explain why, sometimes we find a particular difference more annoying.

Often, when we are dating someone, we just don't notice all those differences that one day we will. Why? It's because most of us are on our best behaviour when we're dating and making an effort to get to know someone. Once we're married we tend to revert to our personality type – so we may have seemed outgoing because we were making the effort to date, but in reality we might prefer quiet evenings in. Good marriage preparation should help us to see some of those differences but most of us have not done that. What can we do to negotiate annoying differences once we are married?

Firstly, take time to understand. Understand why your partner has that difference, is it their personality, the effect of history on them or just their current thinking? You could both take one of the main online personality tests and discuss the results. There are lots out there but we have found the '16 Personality Test' an easy and helpful one to do. Visit https://www.16personalities.com/. This will give you insights and information about yourself and your partner that you can discuss and unpick with each other.

Secondly, take the time to communicate why you're finding this difference challenging. Remember the difference is not an issue unless you make it one. Couples manage to live with big differences about how they like to do things as long as they communicate well with each other.

Thirdly, think about how your differences can complement each other. If one of you is fiery and passionate and the other calm – think about what it would be like if you were both fiery! Or if you were both calm. Each difference has a flip side – learn to see that flip side in your partner. Their fieriness can be the passion you need to create adventure in your marriage. Your calmness may be just what they need to bring stability to children.

Fourthly, think about how you react to each other's differences. Things that seemed 'cute' when you first got married can become irritating the longer you are married. If you find it irritating that your partner is messy, think about how you communicate that. If a guest came into your house and didn't put their shoes on the shoe rack would you speak exasperatedly to them? No, probably not - so just because your partner has been doing this for longer doesn't mean you can be rude to them! Proverbs tells us a quiet word turns away wrath, so a gentle word can achieve more than exasperation.

The reality is that we need our differences – and we get to choose if we let them be barriers to connection, or gifts that enrich our marriage. It is possible to have long happy marriages and have differences!

## Read:

*The human body has many parts, but the many parts make up one whole body. So it is with the body of Christ. Some of us are Jews, some are Gentiles, some are slaves, and some are free. But we have all been baptized into one body by one Spirit, and we all share the same Spirit.*

*Yes, the body has many different parts, not just one part. If the foot says, 'I am not a part of the body because I am not a hand,' that does not make it any less a part of the body. And if the ear says, 'I am not part of the body because I am not an eye,' would that make it any less a part of the body? If the whole body were an eye, how would you hear? Or if your whole body were an ear, how would you smell anything?*

*But our bodies have many parts, and God has put each part just where he wants it. How strange a body would be if it had only one part! Yes, there are many parts, but only one body. The eye can never say to the hand, 'I don't need you.' The head can't say to the feet, 'I don't need you.'*

*In fact, some parts of the body that seem weakest and least important are actually the most necessary. And the parts we regard as less honorable are those we clothe with the greatest care. So we carefully protect those parts that should not be seen, while the more honorable parts do not require this special care. So God has put the body together such that extra honor and care are given to those parts that have less dignity. This makes for harmony among the members, so that all the members care for each other. If one part suffers, all the parts suffer with it, and if one part is honored, all the parts are glad.*

1 Corinthians 12 v 12-26 NLT

## Pray:

That God would show you how the differences you have can work together. Pray for ways to show grace to each other in the areas you find your differences difficult.

## Discuss:

Are there things about each other that used to bug you, but that you've grown to accept, even like? And how about other things you're still having to work on? What can you both do about those?

## Declare:

I celebrate and enjoy that we are each wonderfully and uniquely made. I will understand my differences from other people.

GOING DEEPER

GOING DEEPER

**DAY 25**

# Learning to Laugh

Laughter therapy is something that is being increasingly understood and practiced. Why? Because the world has realised that laughter is good for us. This is something the Bible has always known!

> *When the LORD restored the fortunes of Zion, we were like those who dreamed.*
> *Our mouths were filled with laughter, our tongues with songs of joy.*

PSALM 126 V 1-2A [NIV]

One of the marks of a successful marriage is laughter. Learning to laugh together and to make each other laugh is key to the shared enjoyment of life.

There's some debate that children laugh more than adults, a number of studies show this to be true, others are not so sure. From an observational perspective it can sometimes appear that some adults have forgotten how to laugh. It might sometimes feel that life has got too busy to allow time for laughter but it's really worth making the time, or changing an attitude that suggest that other things are more important than having fun and laughing. It is now proven that there are health benefits to laughter. We tend to laugh most when we're in social interactions, so laughter can benefit our relationship as well as creating moments of shared enjoyment and joy.

A couple that laughs together will often find the humour in a situation instead of being irritated with each other. Laughing at the funny side of a glass of wine being spilt rather than getting cross at one another will help bond us.

Finding things that you can laugh at together, whether that is a funny film, programme or jokes can also bring closeness.

A couple that laughs together can even in the midst of disagreements make each other laugh and this can really help with diffusing a tense moment. It might seem strange if this is not part of your relationship but it can really work.

So maybe stop and allow yourself to see the funny side of life or a situation, then share it with your partner. Even if laughter starts with you laughing at the laughter it's a start! Of course, remember that you are laughing with, and not, at your partner!

## Read:

*When the LORD restored the fortunes of Zion,*
*we were like those who dreamed.*
*Our mouths were filled with laughter,*
*our tongues with songs of joy.*
*Then it was said among the nations,*
*'The LORD has done great things for them.'*
*The LORD has done great things for us,*
*and we are filled with joy.*
*Restore our fortunes, LORD,*
*like streams in the Negev.*
*Those who sow with tears*
*will reap with songs of joy.*
*Those who go out weeping,*
*carrying seed to sow,*
*will return with songs of joy,*
*carrying sheaves with them.*

PSALM 126 NIV

## Pray:

That joy and laughter may be a hallmark of your marriage.

## Discuss:

When did each of you last have a good laugh? When did you last laugh together? Do you find each other funny? Does your relationship need to be "lightened"?

## Declare:

Laughter is good medicine and I will laugh, appropriately, more often. Laughter will be part of my relationship with my partner.

# GOING DEEPER

## DAY 26

# Juggling Roles

How good are you at juggling, at keeping several balls in the air and spinning many plates simultaneously? We have lots of analogies in English for managing a number of things at the same time, it's something many of us live our lives doing, and some of us do it better than others. The important thing to remember in a relationship is that so long as both of you remain within your comfort zone, it doesn't matter how many balls you each juggle or which of you does what.

Why are we making a point about this? It's because expectations and perceptions can so easily get in the way of practicalities and reality, and they really shouldn't. Let us take you back to the first couple of days of this devotional where we were talking about Biblical marriage and the concept of mutual submission. It's actually a far more challenging idea to live out than first meets the eye. Amongst everything else, mutual submission means recognising one's own, and each other's, weaknesses and being able to both admit to these and to step up to and compensate for these in each other within your marriage. Of course in many marriages this is an unspoken process that develops as the relationship matures, but this only really works if mutual submission is at the core of the transaction, because, ultimately, that's what it is.

There's another aspect to this, and this addresses our point about expectations. Historically society has expected that husbands will be the bread winner and that wives will manage the home. A marriage based on mutual submission turns this on its head and says, "You do what you do best and I'll do the same". Mutual submission plays to each other's strengths, which could leave him as a house husband and her out working, and here's the point. It doesn't matter.

It's important to recognise that this concept can be challenging. We've hinted at this before, many men find their identity in their masculine roles, many women do the same, as mothers or home-makers. It's only when these roles become immutable that they challenge the flexibility that mutual submission asks of us. We have to be prepared to compromise for the good of our partners.

We all have balls to juggle, that's the world we live in, but being prepared to compromise, being happy with the balls that you're most able to juggle easily, and making sure your partner is happy too is what makes for a solid marriage.

## Read:

*That is why a man leaves his father and mother and is united to his wife, and they become one flesh.*

GENESIS 2 V 24 NIV

## Pray:

Father God, help me to fulfil my role within our marriage in an way that honours you and my spouse and, Father God, help me to help my spouse to do the same.

## Discuss:

Do you feel that any of the tasks you regularly undertake in your marriage have fallen on you by default or assumption? How would you like to change that? Are there things you do that you feel your partner could do better?

## Declare:

We are one flesh with one aim and purpose. We determine to support each other in this.

GOING DEEPER

DAY 27

# Understanding Your Past

While we don't want to live in our past, we are all affected by it and the only way to truly understand our present is to understand how our past has impacted how we think and feel today. To have a healthy marriage we need to understand how the relationships that made up our lives as a child still affect us.

Reflecting on our childhood, and unpacking whether we saw healthy patterns for marriage is a good place to start. If Mum and Dad stayed together in a long happy marriage where they resolved conflict, then we are going to have a different view on marriage than if our home was full of arguments and instability.

It's not only the pattern of marriage we grew up with that affects us, but also how we were nurtured, or not, by our parents. If we are used to loving, nurturing relationships, then we are more able to be in a loving nurturing relationship ourselves and are likely to seek that out in a partner. If we have had a dysfunctional childhood, then that is going to affect our current relationship.

It does NOT mean that we have to be trapped by the past. Just because we had dysfunction in our childhood does not mean we have to repeat it. We may have feelings of insecurity, pain, fear of rejection or abandonment that we have to face but they can be dealt with!

First of all, recognising that we have feelings of insecurity, pain, rejection, fear or abandonment is a start. Sometimes we only realise they are there when we are in a relationship. It might be that when we have an argument with our partner we feel rejection. Learning to articulate that this is what you are feeling, and understanding that it stems from your past can help you and your partner navigate it.

Secondly, once we have recognised these feelings we need to take responsibility for communicating them to our partner. This can be scary, if we are feeling rejection then telling our partner can be a big risk. What if they reject us too? Ironically this fear can cause us to act in a way that provokes the very thing we are afraid of. Instead, taking the risk and letting our partner know that we are feeling rejection can help them understand.

Thirdly, as you identify areas of your past that affect your current behaviour, take the time to process and understand the implications of these. Whether you do this with a pastoral worker, counsellor, in a Sozo or by yourself/with your partner it doesn't matter, the important thing is that we all keep working on our own inner healing journey.

Understanding your past doesn't have to be a negative experience, it is also about taking the good from it and seeing the strengths that have been passed down to you. Helping your partner understand and appreciate these things about you is also important. You might have had a dysfunctional childhood but that could have left you with determination and focus. Learning to see the positive things from your past is part of the process. As the saying goes, when life gives you lemons, learn to make lemonade. Lemons are the sour things we get in life, but it is possible to make something good out of them. Helping your partner to understand what the lemons were and how you have made lemonade will help the whole process of working through your past and the impact it's been having on your current relationships.

## Read:

*I don't mean to say that I have already achieved these things or that I have already reached perfection. But I press on to possess that perfection for which Christ Jesus first possessed me. No, dear brothers and sisters, I have not achieved it, but I focus on this one thing: Forgetting the past and looking forward to what lies ahead, I press on to reach the end of the race and receive the heavenly prize for which God, through Christ Jesus, is calling us.*

PHILIPPIANS 3 V 12- 13 [NLT]

## Pray:

Ask God to highlight any parts of your past that are affecting your present.

## Discuss:

How do you both see your pasts? Were they happy times for both of you? How much of your pasts have you brought into your present? How does that effect your relationship?

## Declare:

I am not a subject to the past. I have a present and a future shaped and formed by God.

GOING DEEPER

## DAY 28

# Getting Rid of the Victim, Abuser, Hero Cycle

What do we mean by this title? The victim is the person who is looking for someone to rescue them, in a marriage it can look like you wanting your partner to be the one who makes you whole and fulfils ALL your emotional needs. The abuser (or bully) is the person who uses manipulation and control to get their own way and have their needs met; this can look like being emotionally or physically manipulative. If you are the hero, you feel like you need to rescue others and take responsibility for other people's lives in order to meet your own needs. In a marriage this looks like someone who is always doing things for their partner and disempowering them from doing things for themselves.

When we feel powerless we will switch between all three of these roles, none of them healthy, and all of them destructive in the long term to our marriage. Using tactics like withdrawal, silence, nagging, ridicule, tears or anger to manipulate others, or trying to punish others by using any of these are all part of the power play used by victims, abusers and heroes. Heroes will manipulate you by wanting you to be grateful for them rescuing you. When these tactics are used the aim is to gain control because underneath there is fear, anxiety and insecurity.

So what do we do if we recognise these patterns of behaviour in our marriage? First of all we need to recognise and take responsibility for our own part in the process. Powerless people will find it easier to point the finger at their partner and say, "Look that's you – you're the bully, hero or victim, it's not me!". The truth is that if our partner is displaying some of these traits it's quite likely we are too, as powerless people often attract each other.

Secondly, we need to recognise that we cannot control anyone else; on a good day we might be able to control ourselves – but even that can be a challenge! We need to deal with the hurt, insecurity, and fear in our own lives so that we move away from feeling the need to control.

Thirdly, we need to spend some time asking God to reveal to us the lies we're believing that have kept us locked in the victim, hero, abuser triangle. When you discover what the lies are it may be that you need to forgive some people for teaching you, or allowing you to learn these lies, but you also need to repent for having believed them. Repenting, by the way, is more than saying sorry it is changing the way that you think.

Fourthly, we need to change the way we react to life so that instead of becoming infected by the environment and always thinking we're just a victim of our circumstances, we choose instead what our response to them is going to be. Now when we see our partner or anyone else trying to draw us into their sob story, our response is to not be drawn in but to empower them to ask what can they do about the situation.

## Read:

*Beloved friends, what should be our proper response to God's marvellous mercies? I encourage you to surrender yourselves to God to be his sacred, living sacrifices. And live in holiness, experiencing all that delights his heart. For this becomes your genuine expression of worship.*

*Stop imitating the ideals and opinions of the culture around you, but be inwardly transformed by the Holy Spirit through a total reformation of how you think. This will empower you to discern God's will as you live a beautiful life, satisfying and perfect in his eyes.*

ROMANS 12 V 1,2 [TPT]

## Pray:

Spend some time asking Father God to highlight any victim, abuser or hero in you. Ask Him to show you any lies you believe that cause you to act in these ways and to highlight anyone you need to forgive for having introduced these attitudes to you. Repent of the lies you have believed and ask Father God to show you truth instead.

## Discuss:

Most people won't have come across this behavioural cycle before. Is there anything in it you recognise? Think of other couples you know, not to criticise but to recognise these dynamics. Then discuss whether you're aware of these tendencies in each other.

## Declare:

I am a new creation. I am re-formed by His grace and love. I am made to re-present His image.

GOING DEEPER

GOING DEEPER

DAY 29

# Dealing with Seasons in Life

One thing we all know is that, over time, things change. That is not only true of external circumstances but as people we change over the years too. The person we marry today will be quite different in 50 years' time and other things will have changed too. We may have had children or had to cope with childlessness. Changes in health, jobs or losing family members are all likely to happen to us and in some way change us.

Most of us in our wedding vows say something along the lines of:

I, Stuart , take you, Liz, to be my wife (in this case!), to have and to hold from this day forward, for better, for worse, for richer, for poorer, in sickness and in health, to love and to cherish, till death us do part, according to God's holy law, in the presence of God I make this vow.

Beautiful words! But, in reality, we have no idea how they will be tested in the years to come. How do we cope with the changes that come along?

Keeping God at the centre of our marriages means that we have an anchor to hold onto when things change. Even positive changes like children, or a new job or home can bring with them challenges that see us making the choice to put our trust in Him. Like Isaiah says:-

"Surely God is my salvation; I will trust and not be afraid. The Lord, the Lord himself, is my strength and my defence; he has become my salvation." Isaiah 12 v 2 NIV

Another key to surviving change is to keep talking with one another. We tend to presume that we know our spouse, but this can keep us from connecting. Understanding that they, like us, are always developing helps us to appreciate the need to take time to find out what is really on their heart. This is where it is really important to keep the inspirational communication going that we talked about on a Day 4, and to make sure we keep on prioritising our 'A' time.

None of us know how we will cope in different seasons and so we have to give our spouse room to learn and adapt to us as we change. Coping with illness or bereavement can bring a tumult of emotions that we didn't know we had – everything from anger to deep sadness and it's important to recognise this and give space to each other to allow these emotions to be expressed. It's also important to understand that these emotions are not aimed at us.

Learning helpful ways to express emotions and feelings of anger, sadness, grief, hurt or disappointment is important in keeping our connection with our partner. It's okay to say "I am feeling angry about...." But shouting at our partner isn't so helpful!

Understanding how each of you process emotion is vital – some people find it helpful to do something physical when angry, others want to retreat into a cave. Allowing each other the space to do this and then to come together and speak to each to bring understanding will help you survive those tough times.

Strong emotions do not have to be destructive, we have a God who understands, and it is possible to communicate with each other in safe ways too. Most seasons of life bring with them joy and challenges, learning how to cope with the challenges and find the joy can be a key to making the most of them.

# GOING DEEPER

## Read:

*O Lord, help me again! Keep showing me such mercy.*
*For I am in anguish, always in tears,*
*and I'm worn out with weeping.*
*I'm becoming old because of grief; my health is broken.*
*I'm exhausted! My life is spent with sorrow,*
*my years with sighing and sadness.*
*Because of all these troubles, I have no more strength.*
*My inner being is so weak and frail.*
*My enemies say, 'You are nothing!'*
*Even my friends and neighbors hold me in contempt!*
*They dread seeing me*
*and they look the other way when I pass by.*
*I am totally forgotten, buried away like a dead man,*
*discarded like a broken dish thrown in the trash.*
*I overheard their whispered threats, the slander of my*
*enemies.*
*I'm terrified as they plot and scheme to take my life.*
*I'm desperate, Lord! I throw myself upon you,*
*for you alone are my God!*
*My life, my every moment, my destiny—it's all in your*
*hands.*
*So I know you can deliver me*
*from those who persecute me relentlessly.*
*Smile on me, your servant.*
*Let your undying love and glorious grace*
*save me from all this gloom.*

PSALM 31 V 9-16 TPT

## Pray:

Think about the season you are in at the moment in your marriage. What can you give thanks to God for? What emotions does thinking about these things bring up in you that you can share with God together? What do you need to ask for God's help with in this season?

## Discuss:

What's troubling you about the season you personally find yourself in right now, both physically and emotionally? What do you see as being the challenges that the future holds for you? How can your partner help you deal with and get through these?

## Declare:

Emotions are a gift from God. I use my emotions well. I communicate my feelings and thoughts in a manner that build relationship.

DAY 30

# Empathy, Sympathy and Compassion

These are three words that are often used synonymously, as if they have the same meaning, and they really haven't! Very often we can think that being sympathetic is the right thing to be and to do. We can even think that showing sympathy is a Godly reaction to the woes and tragedies of life, but that once we've shown our sympathy to whatever degree the occasion demands, we can move on. Perhaps that's being a little unfair, harsh even, but it's done to amplify a point. We can sympathise sitting on the opposite side of a table to someone. We can only emphasise sitting beside someone. And then there's compassion!

Sympathy says, "I am sorry for you". Empathy says, "I share your pain". Compassion tends to say, "I am sorry for you and want to do something about it." Nowhere is it as important to recognise these differences as in a marriage. We may feel sorry about our spouse's loss of their job, or an illness they have. We may even feel sympathetic and tell them how rough that is and share with them the sorrow we feel for them. We may even feel sorry for ourselves for the way their problem is or will affect us. More often than not, though, it's not sympathy that is needed from us, it's empathy, and empathy often has to be worked on. We don't always feel naturally empathetic, even with those we love. Sometimes we have to work to put ourselves in their shoes both in the way we think and emotionally, so we understand both how they're thinking and how they're feeling. Here's where 'compassion' comes in again. Empathetic compassion is what will then encourage you to take action, to engage with your spouse's pain and actively help.

To be able to sit next to our partner, to put an arm around their shoulders and show them how much we share their pain and distress and want to be with them to work through things is a gift to both and we do this best by asking our partner what would be helpful. Our inclination may be to try and solve their problem, but this can be anything but helpful. Sometimes we don't want to be fixed, we want to be listened to and understood – actually just listening can be the gift we offer best in our marriages.

## Read:

> *Jesus saw the huge crowd as he stepped from the boat, and he had compassion on them and healed their sick.*

JOHN 14 V 14 NLT

> *Rejoice with those who rejoice, and weep with those who weep.*

ROMANS 12:15 NKJV

Looking at how Jesus exemplifies compassion can help us. In John 14, for instance, we see that Jesus had compassion on the crowds and that led him to heal the sick. Often, Jesus takes the time to ask people what is it that they want. In Mark 10 when Jesus meets blind Bartimaeus we would think it is obvious what a blind man needs. However Jesus stops and in Mark 10 v 51 asks Bartimaeus what he wants from him. Why is this important? In those moments when we need compassion from another, we often don't want the solution of someone else's making but in the asking it helps us work out what we need ourselves and helps us move forward in the situation. In a marriage it helps the marriage stay balanced so that one person doesn't become the 'needy one' and the other a rescuer.

## Pray:

Ask Father God if there is anything stopping you showing compassion to your spouse. Ask God to heal this area of your marriage so that you can show compassion.

## Discuss:

Think of times when you have been sympathetic, empathetic or compassionate with each other and how it made a difference in the way that you have related to each other and the situation.

## Declaration:

We declare that we will treat each other with compassion.

# GOING DEEPER

GOING DEEPER

**DAY 31**

# In Sickness and in Health

A couple of days ago we talked about seasons, the effect they can have on our marriage and how to deal with them. One of the big changes that we all have to face is our health changing over the years. We may have married a young, fit, virile person but that isn't how they are going to be in 40 years'. Some of us face the new normal of increasing health issues as we get older, others we will face health crises at other points in life. How do we cope with illness? What does it mean to love one another in sickness and in health?

Building a relationship that will cope with sickness and the struggles that go with it begins with how we've built our foundations before the struggles start. If we wait until we face those challenges to develop the skills to handle them we might struggle. We need to build the foundations of good communication, of understanding each other, and having God as our core in the times of health. For so many of us we 'float' through the healthy times and then struggle when we come to the times of 'illness'. What we build now will affect how we cope then.

Psalm 1 talks about the person who puts his pleasure and passion in God becoming like a tree that flourishes in every season of life. It talks about bearing fruit in every season. The only way we bear fruit in every season is to delight ourselves in following God's ways all the time.

We sometimes have the false idea when we begin our married life that our happily ever after will mean that it's all easy and happy. Life isn't like that, hard things happen, and we will face difficulties, but how we flourish in those times is dependent on how much we are planted in God together.

Keeping God at the centre doesn't mean we deny the feelings that

## GOING DEEPER

happen when we have to cope with illness. It does, however, mean learning to pour out these feelings to God, still acknowledging that He is good even if our experience at that moment doesn't bear that out.

It may even mean having to live in the mystery of caring for our sick partner while praying for their healing and not seeing it yet. Most of us find that a hard tension, we like things to be black and white. We would like it to be 'God is good' and therefore that healing happens immediately, and when that isn't the case we can become discouraged. Being planted in God means that we live in a place of trust even when we don't see the answers to our prayers clearly.

## Read:

1 *What delight comes to the one who follows God's ways!*
  *He won't walk in step with the wicked,*
  *nor share the sinner's way,*
  *nor be found sitting in the scorner's seat.*
2 *His pleasure and passion is remaining true to the Word of*
  *'I Am,'*
  *meditating day and night in the true revelation of light.*
3 *He will be standing firm like a flourishing tree*
  *planted by God's design,*
  *deeply rooted by the brooks of bliss,*
  *bearing fruit in every season of his life.*
  *He is never dry, never fainting,*
  *ever blessed, ever prosperous.*
4 *But how different are the wicked.*
  *All they are is dust in the wind—*
  *driven away to destruction!*
5 *The wicked will not endure the day of judgment,*
  *for God will not defend them.*
  *Nothing they do will succeed or endure for long,*
  *for they have no part with those who walk in truth.*
6 *But how different it is for the righteous!*
  *The Lord embraces their paths as they move forward*
  *while the way of the wicked leads only to doom.*

PSALM 1 TPT

## Pray:

Father God we made the vow to 'love each other in sickness and health', it is only with Your help that we can hold to this promise. Father, gives us love for each other in those times, strength when we feel weak, hope when we feel discouraged, peace when we are afraid. Father God help us to be so planted in you that in those times we bear fruit that brings you glory. Amen.

## Discuss:

How resigned are you to the possibility of illness? What would supporting each other through sickness, or even infirmity, look like for you both?

## Declare:

I live in divine health. I live with mystery. You are always good.

GOING DEEPER

DAY 32

# Love

In the first flush of falling in love most of us feel that it will never end and we will always be in love. It feels indestructible. Unfortunately, feelings of love can come and go. When we are dating and we show each other all our good sides it can be easier to feel in love than it can be when we wake up to the person next to us and they're snoring, with bad breath and grumpy as well.

How do we keep loving our partner? Loving each other takes effort - we have to keep choosing to love the person we married and seeing the best in them. Love is a choice, Kris Vallotton says;

"Don't marry the person you fall in love with. A fall is an accident, not an act of your will. If you fell once, chances are you will fall again for someone else. A great marriage is never an accident, it's a covenantal choice that two people make with each other for life. It's only in the soil of this garden that true love can take root in the hearts of its companions. If you do fall in love make sure you covenant to grow in love because what began as an accident needs to be done on purpose!" [2].

We enter into a covenant when we get married. This is not based on feelings but based on the choices we make to stay together. The feelings are great, and we want to nurture them but we can't base our relationship on them. We need to base our relationship on God as our foundation and the promises we made to each other.

If we nurture our relationship, we will find that the love that grows between us will be far deeper and more satisfying than the first flush of love we had when we first met. It is truly fulfilling to be loved by someone who knows you and you are sharing your life with. How do we move, then, from the first love we have for one another to the deep

[1] Kris Vallotton Facebook 24 March 2014

[2] C.S. Lewis *The Great Divorce* Geoffrey Bliss 1945

GOING DEEPER

love of a lasting relationship? We choose each day to see the good in the person we have chosen to love; even when they are being irritating, we look for the gold. We choose to be vulnerable with our partner so that they can get to know and love the real person that we are.

It's easy for us to say, "I love you" as a throw away comment, with little sentiment or meaning. When was the last time you looked into your spouse's eyes and told them you loved them ? You can even follow that up with what you like about them.

C.S. Lewis said "I am in love and out of it I will not go."[2].

Loving one another is a daily choice. We nurture love by our actions of valuing each other, seeing the best in one another, being the person who encourages our partner, who doesn't focus on fault but on success, who chooses to listen, be honest and be patient.

Seem like a tall order! Thankfully, we have a God of love who can help us!

## Read:

[4] *Love is large and incredibly patient. Love is gentle and consistently kind to all. It refuses to be jealous when blessing comes to someone else. Love does not brag about one's achievements nor inflate its own importance. [5] Love does not traffic in shame and disrespect, nor selfishly seek its own honor. Love is not easily irritated or quick to take offense. [6] Love joyfully celebrates honesty] and finds no delight in what is wrong. [7] Love is a safe place of shelter, for it never stops believing the best for others Love never takes failure as defeat, for it never gives up.*

1 Corinthians 13 v 4-7 [TPT]

## Pray:

Ask Jesus to fill you to overflowing with love so that you can love your partner today. Ask God to show you the way He sees your spouse, and to give you new ways to express your love to them today.

## Declare:

My choices are powerful. I choose the ways of love. My words, actions and thoughts are a blessing to others and myself.

GOING DEEPER

DAY 33

# Understanding Masculinity/ Femininity

What does it mean to be male or female? In a world that seems to have scrapped gender and now talks about gender fluidity as a matter of normality, what does the Bible have to say about ideas of masculinity and femininity ?

We know that God made us male and female in his image.

> *So God created human beings in his own image.*
> *In the image of God he created them;*
> *male and female he created them.*

GENESIS 1 V 27 NLT

This tells us that God chose to make us either male or female and that He has placed within us both male and female characteristics. If God has chosen to differentiate males from females then there must be characteristics of being male or female that are unique to each. We also know that God chose that men and women should rule together;

> *Then God blessed them and said, "Be fruitful and multiply.*
> *Fill the earth and govern it. Reign over the fish in the sea,*
> *the birds in the sky, and all the animals that scurry along*
> *the ground"*

GENESIS 1 V 28 NLT

Being male or female is not about a power game with each other, but seeing that we have complementary giftings in our femininity and

[1] M De Paola et al *Teamwork, Leadership and Gender* Institute of Labour Economics. Germany www.iza.org September 2018

masculinity that when used together bring fruitfulness not just for us as a couple but for those around us.

Could it be that the 'world' has rejected notions of masculinity and femininity because of the unhelpful stereotypes that typify these descriptions? Defining that to be 'a man' you have to be unemotional, strong and fearless, and to be a 'woman' you have to be emotional, weak and love children paints pictures that are both unhelpful and mutually exclusive. We all know that both men and women can be emotional or unemotional, strong or weak, or good with children.

Recognising that we are different, that men and women both have unique gifts to bring to the table and learning to draw on those strengths can help us build a strong marriage. Studies have found that those workplaces that have women tend to demonstrate more teamwork and collaboration, just one of the many strengths that women can bring to what has often been thought of as a male preserve.[1]

The reality is that we were made to complement each other, we are different from each other and that makes us stronger. Let's celebrate and value our masculinity and femininity, and through that create healthy marriages and families.

## Read:

1       *In the same way, you wives must accept the authority of your husbands. Then, even if some refuse to obey the Good News, your godly lives will speak to them without any words. They will be won over* 2 *by observing your pure and reverent lives.*

3       *Don't be concerned about the outward beauty of fancy hairstyles, expensive jewelry, or beautiful clothes.* 4 *You should clothe yourselves instead with the beauty that comes from within, the unfading beauty of a gentle and quiet Spirit, which is so precious to God.* 5 *This is how the holy*

*women of old made themselves beautiful. They put their trust in God and accepted the authority of their husbands. [6] For instance, Sarah obeyed her husband, Abraham, and called him her master. You are her daughters when you do what is right without fear of what your husbands might do.*

[7]    *In the same way, you husbands must give honor to your wives. Treat your wife with understanding as you live together. She may be weaker than you are, but she is your equal partner in God's gift of new life. Treat her as you should so your prayers will not be hindered.*

1 PETER 3 V 1-7 <sup>TPT</sup>

## Pray:

Ask God to show you the strengths that you bring to your marriage through your masculinity or femininity. Give thanks for these strengths and how they work together to benefit you both.

## Discuss:

How do you feel about the stereotype of your gender? Do you feel it fits? How would you like to change it?

## Declare:

I am strong and secure in my gender identity. I bring my strengths to my relationship and accept the areas where my partner complements my weaknesses.

GOING DEEPER

GOING DEEPER

DAY 34

# Understanding Roles

At the beginning of this devotional we spent a couple of days talking about the meaning of Biblical marriage. Did this leave you wondering about this applied to your own marriage? The idea of submission to Jesus being our start point for the same relationship husband to wife, wife to husband? It's an idea, a concept, that can take a bit of getting used to, no matter how equally shared you consider your marriage to be at the moment.

That T.D. Jakes quote we gave you, that "No woman wants to be in submission to a man who isn't in submission to God!" is so challenging to husbands trying to understand and establish their role in the 21st Century.

What does it mean to be a man anyway?

It's a question that gnaws at the very foundations of our society. Man as the conqueror, the wage earner and bread winner, presumed provider and unquestioned head of the family is a concept that is laughed at in much of modern society as women, rightly, flex and release their ability to be on a par with their menfolk in all but the most physical of worlds. There's a sense in which men have been left gasping as they try and re-find their feet on the shifting sands of equality, with women proving themselves to be so much more adept at responding with emotional intelligence to the challenges of life and business.

Of course there's also the other side of that coin. The fact that many women have proved themselves to be extraordinarily capable has given rise to the expectation that all women want to be and are capable of becoming "super-mums", running home, children and business with skilful equanimity. How challenging for both wife and husband!

How refreshing then, to have a Godly perspective on how we should order that most important of relationships between men and women, marriage. And how natural and simple it is. If you give me all of you, I'll give you all of me. Put another way, you can trust me to do everything I am capable of doing in and with my life for your benefit and I know I can trust you to do exactly the same for me. Now, how you do that in the day to day is another conversation, but there's no misunderstanding the foundation on which Christian marriage is built.

In the past roles have been a discussion about who does what – but if we start with the principles of honour, submission and devotion then we will find it easier to work out the practicalities of how to apply this in a way that suits your relationship perfectly.

## Read:

[1] *And now let me speak to the wives. Be devoted to your own husbands, so that even if some of them do not obey the Word of God, your kind conduct may win them over without you saying a thing. [2] For when they observe your pure, godly life before God, it will impact them deeply. [3–4] Let your true beauty come from your inner personality, not a focus on the external. For lasting beauty comes from a gentle and peaceful spirit, which is precious in God's sight and is much more important than the outward adornment of elaborate hair, jewelry, and fine clothes.*

[5] *Holy women of long ago who had set their hopes in God beautified themselves with lives lived in deference to their own husbands' authority. [6] For example, our "mother," Sarah, devoted herself to her husband, Abraham, and even called him "master." And you have become her daughters when you do what is right without fear and intimidation.*

> [7] *Husbands, you in turn must treat your wives with tenderness, viewing them as feminine partners who deserve to be honored, for they are co-heirs with you of the "divine grace of life," so that nothing will hinder your prayers.*
>
> 1 Peter 3 v 1-7 [TPT]

## Pray:

Ask Father God to show what roles he wants you to take in your marriage.

## Discuss:

Have you been holding onto certain roles in marriage because you thought you had to? If you re-look at roles with the eyes of honour, submission and devotion to each other does it change things?

## Declaration:

Our marriage will be a place where we can both flourish and grow, where we value each other's roles.

GOING DEEPER

GOING DEEPER

**DAY 35**

# Respect and Honour

We want our marriage to be a place of honour and respect, but we can't demand this. By giving honour to those around us we begin to create the environment for people to give us honour too. Our attitude and actions towards someone show how much honour we give them. Familiarity can stop us giving honour to someone. The person who deserves most honour from us is our spouse. We show that honour not just in how we speak to them but also how we talk about them when we speak to others. In our culture men, when they are with other men, or women, with other women, moan about their spouse or join in with sexist comments about them. Most of us will have been around those conversations where men are put down by their wives or women by their husbands, this is NOT honour! Honour builds up and speaks well of the spouse even, maybe especially when they are not present.

> *Those who control their tongue will have a long life; opening your mouth can ruin everything.*

PROVERBS 13 V 3 NLT

We might be feeling a bit fed up with our spouse, but if we speak negatively about them we dishonour them. Joining in with the moaning of others can dishonour our spouse.

Some people do this in front of others when their spouse is around. This can be just a way of trying to recruit people to our point of view and can be humiliating our spouse. If we have an issue with our spouse the honouring way to deal with it is to speak directly to them in private. If we tried this and feel we haven't got anywhere then we can ask a trusted pastoral worker or counsellor to help us.

Even the way we joke about our spouse in front of others can show if we are being honouring. We may find it amusing to mention that funny little habit they have to others, but does it make them feel valued? Or is it really just a way of making us feel a little smug or big?

We have to remember that honour is about seeing the other person as how God made them and the destiny He has for them, rather than the temporary irritation we feel. I don't honour you because you are perfect I honour you because you are made in God's image for a purpose.

Let's have a think about how we feel honoured by others. Is that how we treat our spouse? Is there anything that we need to apologise to them for ? Do you need to think about what might, in you, make you feel the need to dishonour others?

## Read:

*As the Scriptures say, 'A man leaves his father and mother and is joined to his wife, and the two are united into one.' This is a great mystery, but it is an illustration of the way Christ and the church are one. So again I say, each man must love his wife as he loves himself, and the wife must respect her husband."*

*In Ephesians Paul tells men to love their wives as they love themselves; this follows Jesus' teaching that we will be treated as we treat others. It's clear the Bible wants us to treat others well and with love. Men, if this is a struggle then do you need to spend time making sure that you know and feel God's love for yourself, so that you can love your wife in the same way and to the same depth? Women, you are told to respect your husbands. Paul was giving wives a big clue, if you want to be honoured and respected in your home, then you need to start with respecting your husband.*

EPHESIANS 5 V 31-33 TPT

*Do not judge others, and you will not be judged. For you
will be treated as you treat others. The standard you use in
judging is the standard by which you will be judged.*

*And why worry about a speck in your friend's eye when
you have a log in your own? How can you think of saying
to your friend, 'Let me help you get rid of that speck in
your eye,' when you can't see past the log in your own eye?
Hypocrite! First get rid of the log in your own eye; then
you will see well enough to deal with the speck in your
friend's eye.*

*Don't waste what is holy on people who are unholy. Don't
throw your pearls to pigs! They will trample the pearls, then
turn and attack you.*

MATTHEW 7 V 1-7 NLT

## Pray:

Ask God to show you both anything in your heart that has stopped you
honouring each other. Ask Him and each other for forgiveness for the
times you have dishonoured each other. Pray for Holy Spirit to prompt
you to honour each other in new ways.

## Discuss:

Do you ever feel that your spouse is having a dig ay you when you're with
friends? Have you ever used the safety of company to do the same. Why
did you do it? How did it make you feel?

## Declare:

I am an honourable person. I honour others and show it in my words,
thoughts and actions.

GOING DEEPER

## DAY 36

# Vision and Purpose

We might think that vision and purpose have little to do with our relationship or marriage. It's not true! There is a reason that God has brought the two of you together that is bigger than just you and meeting your needs. This will include any children that you have but is bigger than having children too!

If you were asked, "What's the purpose of your marriage?" what would you say? Having asked this in different settings and seminars we know that people often answer with, "Creating security for each other and children", "being a place of love" or "to make each other happy". These may all be part of marriage for you but they are unlikely to be the big purpose that God has brought you together for.

We want you to ask the question - why has God brought us together? If you spend some time praying about this together hopefully you will begin to get some key words that describe your big purpose – maybe words like pioneers, healers, restorers or hope-bringers.

Then, once you have found your joint purpose, you can begin to ask God "What should this look like for us in our marriage?" The answer to this question will provide your vision. More than one couple may have the word 'pioneer' but for one couple that will look like pioneering in releasing people from bondage through anti-trafficking and for another it could be that they are pioneering by being business entrepreneurs.

Of course you may be wondering what's the point of this exercise and why you should go to the effort of working out your purpose and vision. The answer is that it really helps you to be strategic about your life and what you spend your time, money and effort on. All us of are bombarded by decisions each day; if you have a sense of purpose together then you can decide how you want to focus your energies.

Proverbs 29 v 18 [NASB] says

> *Where there is no vision, the people are unrestrained,*
> *But happy is he who keeps the law.*

We need purpose and vision to give us direction for our lives. A mutual sense of purpose can also help us join together in making it work. Otherwise we can be like two oxen pulling the yoke in different directions – painful and very frustrating!

## Read:

> 'For I know the plans that I have for you,' declares the LORD, 'plans for welfare and not for calamity to give you a future and a hope. Then you will call upon Me and come and pray to Me, and I will listen to you. You will seek Me and find Me when you search for Me with all your heart. I will be found by you,' declares the LORD, 'and I will restore your fortunes and will gather you from all the nations and from all the places where I have driven you,' declares the LORD, 'and I will bring you back to the place from where I sent you into exile.'
>
> JEREMIAH 29 V 11 –14 NASB

## Pray:

Together ask God to show you the purpose He has for your marriage.

## Discuss:

Have either of you considered the question of purpose before? If so, what is/was it? Has it changed? If you've now prayed together about your purpose, what difference will adhering to this purpose make to your lives?

## Declare:

My marriage has a purpose. We will live in and from the purpose the Lord has for us.

GOING DEEPER

GOING DEEPER

DAY 37

# Dreaming Together

Dreaming together is not about having a wild fantasy life but about dreaming about the life you have and will have together.

> *It is pleasant to see dreams come true, but fools refuse to turn from evil to attain them.*

PROVERBS 13 V 19 NLT

We all have dreams, dreams of what it will look like to be together, grow old together, have children together, be a family, what our next home will look like, what jobs we will have or places that we will go. If we don't share these dreams then they can easily turn into disappointments that block our relationship. How can our spouse partner with us to see dreams fulfilled if we don't share them?

Instead we can have the joy of sharing the dreams we have and together seeing them come true. Learning to ask about our dreams can be part of our inspirational communication, drawing out the dreams that lie dormant in each other's hearts.

Maybe you have not allowed yourselves to dream before, if not now is the time to start sharing. Dreams don't just turn into reality on their own we have to do something to partner with them to make them happen. As Proverbs says, the fool refuses to turn from evil to attain them. We may not feel we are doing evil but it does show us that effort needs to be put into the attainment. We need to turn from things we are doing to make the choices that will allow our dreams to come true.

Learning to share these dreams out with each other and then allowing these dreams to be something that you both can join in with can be a fulfilling process that deepens your connection.

We can involve God in this process too, having a dream that the two of you aim for together might be fun but having one that can only be accomplished with God's help is another level of adventure altogether.

## Read:

> *A person may have many ideas concerning God's plan for his life, but only the designs of his purpose will succeed in the end.*
>
> PROVERBS 19 V 21 [TPT]

## Pray:

For God to stir up new dreams in you for you to accomplish together with Him.

## Discuss:

What dreams have you already realised in your life? Which ones wait to be fulfilled? How do your dreams fit in with the purpose we looked at yesterday? What needs to change to see them match?

## Declare:

I live with and from Godly dreams that I share with Him and my partner.

GOING DEEPER

DAY 38

# Choosing the "Us" and Still Being "You"

God has made us as unique individuals; it's a complete mystery how we become one in marriage and yet still bring our uniqueness to the marriage.

Some married couples seem completely subsumed by each other, other couples lead very separate lives. Both these could be seen being at the extreme ends of the relational spectrum, so how do we walk the balance where we choose 'us' and yet still remain ourselves?

It could be that in some areas of married life we find it easy to be together and remain ourselves but in others we struggle. It may be that one of us is more confident, dominant or less flexible so the other easily yields and in doing so loses their own identity.

Learning to reflect on how we value our partner's uniqueness in our marriage and to consider if we, in any way, stop them from being all that they can should be a constant consideration. What were the qualities in your partner that attracted you to them? Do you still give room for them to express those qualities today?

We have to prioritise our marriage above other relationships but that doesn't mean we have to do so in a suffocating way. It may be that your partner has a hobby or interest that you don't share, how do you give space for this? Or have you let your hobby or interest dominate the relationship so that there isn't time or space for each other.

Learning to keep being you is about being willing to keep asking these sorts of questions of yourself and each other. Does one of you always

145

make the plans for what you are doing or do you both have input? Remember silence when making decisions is still making a choice! You need to speak up if you want your desires to be part of the process.

Paul in Philippians talks about humility creating the atmosphere where you put others first. If you both choose to put each other first then you will create the place where you can be uniquely you and yet together.

## Read:

2    *So I'm asking you, my friends, that you be joined together in perfect unity—with one heart, one passion, and united in one love. Walk together with one harmonious purpose and you will fill my heart with unbounded joy.*

3    *Be free from pride-filled opinions, for they will only harm your cherished unity. Don't allow self-promotion to hide in your hearts, but in authentic humility put others first and view others as more important than yourselves. 4 Abandon every display of selfishness. Possess a greater concern for what matters to others instead of your own interests. 5 And consider the example that Jesus, the Anointed One, has set before us. Let his mindset become your motivation.*

6    *He existed in the form of God, yet he gave no thought to seizing equality with God as his supreme prize. Instead he emptied himself of his outward glory by reducing himself to the form of a lowly servant. He became human! 8 He humbled himself and became vulnerable, choosing to be revealed as a man and was obedient. He was a perfect example, even in his death—a criminal's death by crucifixion!*

9    *Because of that obedience, God exalted him and multiplied his greatness! He has now been given the greatest of all names!*

> <sup>10</sup> *The authority of the name of Jesus causes every knee to bow in reverence! Everything and everyone will one day submit to this name—in the heavenly realm, in the earthly realm, and in the demonic realm. <sup>11</sup> And every tongue will proclaim in every language: "Jesus Christ is Lord Yahweh," bringing glory and honor to God, his Father!"*
>
> PHILIPPIANS 2 V 2-11 <sup>TPT</sup>

## Pray:

Father God, show us how we can be the individuals you have made us to be and yet be united together in marriage. Teach us through Jesus example to create an atmosphere of humility that allows each of us to grow and be all you have called us to be. Thank you for making us unique and bringing us together in marriage.

## Discuss:

How much do you both feel you've compromised your interests and hobbies for the sake of your marriage? Is there a way you can give each other the freedom to re-engage with any of these? How would that make you both feel?

## Declare:

I delight in being me. I delight in being part of "us". We together are more than the sum of the parts.

GOING DEEPER

**DAY 39**

# 'Til Death Do Us Part

You don't need us to tell you that marriage is a lifelong commitment and not one to be taken on lightly. Marriage can be fulfilling, full of pleasure and bring us security but it can also be one that brings pain, hurt and sadness.

We hope that by using the tools we've discussed over the last month or so that your marriage will grow and develop. We want you to have a marriage that withstands the storms of life and brings you great joy too.

For this to happen and to have a marriage that lasts until death we believe that God's help, a good community of fellow Christians around us and, at times, help from outsiders like counsellors, pastors or Sozo for Couples is vital. It's not a failure to ask for help, none of us think it is a failure to go to a doctor when we are sick but many of us feel that it is if we ask for help in our marriage.

Sometimes we become so embroiled in a situation that we can't see what we need to deal with it or work out a solution to overcome it. Many years' experience in helping married couples have taught us that couples often leave it too late to come for that help.

What makes a good marriage? God in the centre, good communication, laughter, understanding each other well and a joint sense of purpose and vision are some of the main elements. It's not the size of your house, where you end up living, how many children you do or don't have or your success in careers that will determine your success in marriage!

## Read:

*Unless the LORD builds a house,*
*the work of the builders is wasted.*

*Unless the LORD protects a city,*
*guarding it with sentries will do no good.*

PSALM 127 V 1-2 <sup>NLT</sup>

## Pray:

Come before God and thank him for your marriage and each other. Ask Holy Spirit to show you areas of your marriage that you need to keep bringing to Him and work on together. Ask Him to keep your hearts soft.

## Discuss:

How has this month-long journey *Going Deeper* been for you both? What have you learned? How will your marriage be different? What next?

## Declare :

My marriage is life long and goes from strength to strength.

GOING DEEPER

GOING DEEPER

**DAY 40**

# What's Next?

What's next? We hope that you have enjoyed this devotional book and that it has deepened your connection with each other and God. What we've found is that couples often need a door opening excuse to start discussing things that might have been on their minds for years, the elephants in their relationship, and we hope that working through this together will have brought some of these to the surface.

You may also have found that some areas in your marriage have been highlighted and realise you could do with a little help and we would encourage you to not ignore this. Why not visit the Sozo for Couples website, www.sozoforocouples.org, and read some of the testimonials from couples who have found a Sozo for Couples' session helpful. Then book in! Sessions are mostly online, but can also be in person if that's preferred.

We've also included a list of recommended additional reading. If you recognise a need to grow in one specific area such as communication, boundaries or sexual intimacy – then have a look at the books we suggest and use these as resources to help you.

It is so important to recognise that marriage is not static. As with so many of the important things in life you are always either growing together or growing apart, you may think that you've reached or achieved a plateau of consistency, in your marriage but the truth is that if that's you it's because you've recognised, consciously or unconsciously, that growing together takes a constant investment of energy, commitment, and courage. The rewards of your investment are huge as you both enjoy the benefits of marriage intimacy, security, fun and companionship.

If the idea of investing in your marriage makes sense then why not aim to pick up this devotional again in a couple of years' time and work through it again, reviewing whether you've been doing the things that you've changed or if you've quietly slipped back into old habits. If you have, give yourselves grace and try again. It might be worth praying through why you slipped back.

What we do know is that the tools that are contained within the pages of this devotional can help you have a marriage that is lasting, fulfilling and fun!

We pray that you may know:

> *I know my lover is mine and I have everything in you, for we delight ourselves in each other.*

SONG OF SONG 2 v 16 TPT

## APPENDIX I

# Types of Communication. .

We have identified three levels of communication in a couple's relationship. Every relationship needs each of these levels to make it fulfilling and to make us feel connected with each other.

**Informational**: This is the kind of communication most of us do on a daily basis. We tell our partner when we are going to work, chat about who needs to pick up the kids or put out the bins. It's the day-in and day-out conversation that makes up a lot of what we say. It is important for the communication and exchange of information but does not connect us on a deeper level.

**Intermediate**: This communication is more about what we might be thinking or planning in the next six months or year. What holidays we are going to take, plans for work, how to manage our money from month to month.

**Inspirational**: This communication meets our deeper need to be heard and understood. In this communication, we speak about our hopes and dreams and our deep thoughts about feelings and issues. We listen to our partner and reflect on their thoughts. Understanding our partner at this deeper level will affect the choices we make at the intermediate and informational levels of communication. This is where we are vulnerable and open. Asking questions like "Where would you like to be in five years?" and "What would you do with a £/$1m?" can help this communication.

There are any number of questions that a couple can ask of each other to encourage the inspirational level of communication. It's usually best if, once asked, the couple spend some time answering separately before coming together to discuss. Here are a few:

GOING DEEPER

1. Can you identify if you do all three types of communication as a couple? When do you do them.

2. What would help improve the depth of communication you have at all levels?

3. What would help you to feel more listened to at each level?

4. What can you do to improve your communication?

GOING DEEPER

**APPENDIX II**

# Building Values.

How do you as a couple want to be defined?

Our purpose, vision and values should underpin and determine what kind of marriage we have. As a couple it's important to build values that you share and live from.

Understanding what values are important to you should affect your choices and reduce conflict. For example, if we have decided that we have a value on hospitality and that we will work this out by inviting people to our home for Sunday lunch, we cannot then be upset when people are in our home!

Here are some questions to help you determine your values as a couple. Complete them separately and then come together to discuss. your answers:

1. What values did you see in the home where you grew up? How were these acted out?

2. If you were to write a vision statement for you as a couple what would it be?

155

# GOING DEEPER

3.    What values will help you to implement this? What values do you have regarding:

- Your relationship

- Your family (both children and extended family)

- Your priorities over work/ leisure/ finances

- Your relationship with God, separately and together Your Church

4.  Now you have identified your values as a couple how will you practically work this out?

# Resources

Dr. Gary Chapman *The Five Love Languages*

John Gottman *The Seven Principles for Making Marriage Work*

Danny Silk *Keep Your Love On*

Stephen de Silva *Money and the Prosperous Soul*

Tim LaHay, Beverly LaHay *The Act of Marriage; the beauty of sexual love*

Darrell Cocup, Liz Gregg *Starting Out*

Darrell Cocup, Anthea Cocup, Liz Gregg *The Sozo for Couples Manual*

To book a Sozo for Couples and to find our more visit www.sozoforcouples.org

GOING DEEPER

Printed in Great Britain
by Amazon